*"A second collection of unusual encounters and happenings found throughout our County in unexpected places."*
—Fred Dorsey, historic preservationist

*"Jilted lovers and vengeful spirits, murder and mayhem. Phantasms, ghosts, and apparitions of every kind woven into fantastic re-tellings of local hauntings, real and imaginary. And that's just the first few pages! These stories are not displayed in a museum case, they come down through generations of story-telling, and with each generation, the spirits become more horrifying! A great addition to the library of anyone interested in local history, especially the haunted history."*
—Wiley Purkey, artist, author and historian

*"I love the instances, like the chapter on The Meade House, where the results of our paranormal investigation confirms or adds to the historical research on the property. This book is a great combination of the history of the buildings and the people who lived and died in them and accounts of supernatural phenomena that gives a window into the afterlife."*
—Olen Prince, founder, Dead of Night Paranormal Investigations

*"Shelley Davies Wygant tells great ghost stories but she doesn't stop there. She wraps the places they haunt in such a full and detailed history that you can see these places as they were centuries ago, with the spirits of the people who used to live there, and who stayed around after they died. It's a great gift to see the centuries roll away from places you pass every day, and it's a gift that Ms. Wygant shares with all her readers. Be prepared to see Howard County with a new pair of eyes—it won't look quite the same after you read this book."*
—Matt Lake, author of Weird Maryland

# HAUNTED
## HOWARD COUNTY, MARYLAND

**SHELLEY DAVIES WYGANT**

Haunted
America

Published by Haunted America
A Division of The History Press
Charleston, SC
www.historypress.com

*Front cover*: Al Hafner.
*Back cover*: Howard County Historical Society; *inset*: Howard County Department of Recreation & Parks.

First published 2021

Manufactured in the United States

ISBN 9781467147149

Library of Congress Control Number: 2021938363

*Notice*: The information in this book is true and complete to the best of our knowledge. It is offered without guarantee on the part of the author or The History Press. The author and The History Press disclaim all liability in connection with the use of this book.

*Dedicated to the recently revealed, nearly forgotten and yet-to-be-discovered ghosts of Howard County.*

# CONTENTS

# Contents

# ACKNOWLEDGEMENTS

After researching and writing *Haunted Ellicott City*, I thought I had pretty much wrung out every supernatural story the area had to tell. But I couldn't have been more wrong. As I began digging around in archives and asking old-timers what they knew, tales of other Howard County ghosts and their haunts began to materialize before me.

Some, like the seemingly endless supply of specters flitting through the halls and workrooms of Belmont Manor and Savage Mill, have been well documented—although they still have secrets to reveal. Others, like the "Blue Lady" of Salopha, the lovelorn ghost at the Grayhouse and the spirit of a violently murdered woman that still lingers on the site of the Gerwig-Lintner House, were little known but nevertheless had the power to surprise, intrigue and shock. There were so many that I literally ran out of room to include them all. Another Howard County ghost book may be in the offing.

This book could not have been written without the help of some very special people and organizations, including the following:

All of the authors of past books and articles on the supernatural, individual tellers of tales of encounters with ghosts and all other sources of accounts of the spirit world that I have drawn from to create this comprehensive compilation of ghost stories that have floated around since the earliest days of Howard County.

Jeffrey Wygant, my husband, best friend and unfailing supporter of all of my odd and inspired adventures; Lara Westwood, librarian, Maryland Historical Trust, who unfailing honored my requests for "just one more picture"; Paulette Lutz, deputy director of the Howard County Historical Society; Fred Dorsey, local historian, preservationist and friend.

Thanks also to Steve McKenna, who shared his haunted house and served as my ace editor and eagle-eyed proofreader; and to proofer and friend Carole Nicotera-Ward.

Last but certainly not least, I am deeply grateful to all of the present and past residents of Howard County who shared their supernatural experiences, haunted houses, family histories, personal photographs, recollections on Facebook and moral support with me, including:

Karen Zell Campbell, Casey Caulder, Jennifer Chandler-Nesbitt, Shari Lynn White Fant, Harvey Goolsby, Mark Greenwald, Patricia Emard Greenwald, Karen Griffith, Georgia Hatcher, Shannon Renee Hughes, Michael Kuegler, Jeffrey Lewis, Anthony Maccherone, Donna Mathias-Hoffman, Pat Nash, Doug Rowe, Karen Schmincke-Militano, Lisa Schmidt, Diane Schulte, Anne Schoenhutt, Pete Shinnamon, John Strott, Albert Gallatin Warfield III, Missy Warfield, Ashley Serio West and Chuck Zepp. Forgive me if I left anyone out.

This book literally couldn't have been written without you.

# INTRODUCTION

*Howard County…the innumerable springs of clear cold water that leap up rejoicingly everywhere from its boom, it's wooded hillsides and green valleys.*
*—G.M. Hopkins, civil engineer in his celebrated Atlas of 1878*

C arved off of the northwest end of Anne Arundel County in the mid-nineteenth century, the bucolic, 251-square-mile tract of land that became Maryland's second-smallest county is nevertheless packed border to border with agricultural, industrial and colonial political history—and apparently, ghosts.

Until the 1600s, Howard County was home only to wildlife and Native American peoples who had arrived in the area more than ten thousand years earlier. Farmers and hunters, these indigenous people were primarily from the Algonquin tribes; however, there were also Iroquois and Siouan people living here.

All that changed in 1608, when an Englishman, Captain John Smith of Jamestown, made his way up the Patapsco River in his extensive exploring and mapping efforts of the Chesapeake Bay and its tributaries. Howard County's history begins nearly eighty years later, in 1687, when a Puritan colonial-settler named Adam Shipley received the county's first land grant from Lord Baltimore. Patented as "Adam the First," the five-hundred-acre tract was located near Ellicott City.

During the colonial period in America, a governor or proprietary could sell or give away land to soldiers and farmers as compensation for their military service or aid in settling the land. The area encompassing Howard County originally had 359 land grants. In most cases, their names referenced the land-grant owner, but in many others, these tracts of land were given much more fanciful and entertaining designations.

Patent names like "Ranter's Ridge," "The Mistake," "Lost by Neglect" and "Hard to Get Dear Paid For" can be found tucked in the nooks and crannies among Howard County land-ownership records. A few were huge—eleven were over two thousand acres. Most others were much smaller, totaling less than one hundred acres. Legend has it that for some of the county's wealthiest citizens, the smaller grants were so inconsequential to their owners that they were sometimes won and lost in card games.

Among the largest was the seven-thousand-acre "Doughoregan Manor," a tract that Charles Carroll "The Settler" acquired in 1702. His son Charles Carroll "The Signer" went on to become one of the signatories to the Declaration of Independence and the only Catholic to do so.

Other notable milestones in Howard County history are the founding of Ellicotts Mills, later known as Ellicott City in 1772 by the Ellicott brothers from Bucks County, Pennsylvania. It was they who built the first flouring mills on the Patapsco and helped the agriculture transition from tobacco to growing wheat. They also established the beginnings of the National Road, whose initial six miles or so ran from Ellicott City to Doughoregan Manor so Carroll could bring his wheat into town to be ground at the mill.

Savage Mill was built on the Patuxent River in 1822 and operated as a textile manufacturing plant until the middle of the twentieth century. In 1830, the Baltimore & Ohio Railroad established the first railroad terminus at Ellicotts Mills, connecting the town to Baltimore. Along those thirteen miles of track, the trains ran across the Thomas Viaduct, the first curved stone-arch bridge in the United States, built near Elkridge in 1835.

In 1839, the area was designated as the Howard District of Anne Arundel County, which officially became the independent jurisdiction of Howard County in 1851. Towns like Lisbon, a supply depot and summer resort, began popping up along the National Road, which was then known as the Old Frederick Turnpike. In the late 1800s, the bustling little town of Clarksville at the junction of Route 32 and Route 108 came to be.

When the Civil War broke out, the county was divided in its sympathies as to the North and South. The railroad and bridges became targets of the Confederate army. Meanwhile, in Cooksville, on Route 97, Confederate general J.E.B. Stuart got waylaid en route to the Battle of Gettysburg by a skirmish with Union troops. He captured them, but the delay was enough to prevent him from getting to the battle in time to help avert the Confederate loss.

For just over one hundred years after the Civil War ended, Howard County remained a sleepy little agricultural county populated by farmers and peppered with fine estates of the home-grown landed gentry and country homes of wealthy outsiders. That all changed in 1966, when construction started on the new town of Columbia, developed by James Rouse and his Rouse Company. In the years prior, Rouse had secretly bought up more than fourteen thousand acres to build a progressive new kind of city designed to integrate the conveniences of commercial establishments like shopping centers and offices into the traditional subdivision design by creating a cluster of "villages." In addition to the creation of a more convenient environment, the core idea was to eliminate racial, religious and class segregation.

Today, although the area retains its agricultural feel, especially in the western part, Howard County has become more developed. Countless historic homesteads have been torn down. Sprawling, hundred-acre farms have been subdivided to create upscale neighborhoods. Yet, the county retains much of its charm and allure. Home to a highly educated population of well over 300,000 people and growing, Howard County ranks among the wealthiest counties in the nation and consistently ranks in the top ten of the best places to live in America.

# PART I

# EASTERN ENTITIES

# 1
# AVOCA

## ELLICOTT CITY

*The ghost of "Emily" is laid to rest as a case of mistaken identity is finally solved.*

Hidden in the deep shadows of its heavily wooded front yard, the imposing granite mansion known as Avoca is a little-known local landmark, despite sitting a scant fifty yards or so from cars whizzing by its location at 4824 Montgomery Road. Later referred to as the Vineyards, the hand-hewn stone house was home to just three families during its approximately 220-year history, with parents passing down the property to their sons or daughters. It is also said to be haunted by a "ghost" who wasn't quite dead yet when she appeared to the last family who owned it.

## THE HISTORY

The house that would eventually be known as Avoca sits on just 5.37 acres of the original 1,000-plus-acre plot that had been patented by Samuel Chew in 1695 as "Chews Resolution Manor" and "Chews Vineyard." Based on the date of the land grant, the tract may have been patented by Samuel L. Chew, grandson of John "Chewe," one of Maryland's original colonists at Jamestown.

In those days, it was not uncommon for wealthy Maryland families to own land grants across the state that they rarely if ever visited, let alone built houses on. The Chew land may have remained vacant until the early 1800s, when young Dr. Arthur William Pue and his wife, Rebecca Ridgely Buchanan—who was also his cousin—purchased about 1,200 acres and began building their handsome stone home.

The three-story-high, one-room-deep front section of the house that faces Montgomery Road is believed to have been built between 1802 and 1810. After getting married in 1800, it's said the Pues welcomed a total of eleven children into their family. Among them were Rebecca Anna, born in 1801, followed by Michael in 1803, Arthur William Jr. in 1804, Charles Ridgely in 1805, Mary in 1806 and Henry Hill in 1810. In 1813, their son Mortimer arrived. Daughters Priscilla Hill and Sophia came along in 1817 and 1818, respectively. While the Pues maintained Avoca as a country home, they also had a house and likely a doctor's office in Baltimore, since their last two daughters, Maria Ridgely and Eliza, were born in the city in 1819 and 1825, respectively.

The large home, with its gracious parlors, roomy bedrooms and cavernous attic, must have been a grand place to grow up, while the endless acres of forest and fields offered unlimited opportunities for adventure and play.

But life for the Pues was not free of sorrow. The year 1844 was a terrible one, bringing the death of two of the daughters, Mary, thirty-eight, and Sophia, twenty-six, who died just a year after getting married. Three years later, Arthur Pue Sr. died, and in 1853, Rebecca departed this life. But the house would live on in the Pue family—at least for a while.

When Dr. Pue died in 1847, his will divvied up the property among his surviving children. Michael, who also became a doctor, and his sister Pricilla got 500.25 acres along with the house and outbuildings, all of which were valued at $2,900 in the 1849 tax assessment. Michael bought his sister out and quickly put the property up for sale. When he couldn't get the price he wanted, he decided to keep the home and land. He lived there with his fellow bachelor brother Mortimer and continued to run the farm.

The 1850 U.S. Census shows Michael owning six enslaved people, including two men, a woman and two boys aged thirteen and eight, as well as a little three-year-old girl. It also indicated that they had five horses, eight milk cows, four head of cattle, thirty hogs and fifteen sheep, and that they grew wheat, rye and corn. In 1858, a tornado ripped through and seriously damaged the barn.

Since neither brother had children to leave the land to, Dr. Pue began slowly selling off some of the land. The year 1877 marked the end of Pue's life and the family's ownership of the home.

The Victorian-era porch has since been replaced by a small portico. *Georgia Wilbur Hatch, Emily's daughter and Emma's great-granddaughter.*

On April 4, 1877, the house, 178 acres of property, every stick of furniture and most of the livestock were sold to Alfred Valentine Thomas for $13,600. He also bought an additional 110 acres that had once been part of the farm.

The sales notice for the property described the land as being "on the road from the Columbia Turnpike to Elkridge Landing and to Waterloo at the terminus of the 'New Cut Road.'…The neighborhood is noted for the salubrity of its climate, the beauty of its scenery, and the culture and elegance of its residents. Mrs. Comfort W. Dorsey, Messrs. James Clark, John C. White, Henry Winter, I. Monroe Mercer, and Captain Jonett U.S. Navy, are among the nearest neighbors."

The new owner, Alfred V. Thomas, thirty-five, was the son of David Ogle Thomas of Rose Hill in Frederick County. Alfred and his wife, Emma Ward Clark, had been married in 1874 just down the road at Wheatfield. They soon settled into the homestead. Alfred named the home Avoca, perhaps as a nod to his initials (A.V.).

Apparently, the couple was very happy in their new home, because nine months later, on February 1, 1878, they welcomed their son James Clark into their little family. In 1881, their daughter Margaret was born, and in 1885, another daughter joined them.

During their time at Avoca, Thomas greatly expanded and improved the home by converting the old kitchen into a dining room and adding a new kitchen at the rear of the house. He also enlarged the second story by raising the chamber over the old kitchen and adding two smaller rooms over the new kitchen to house the servants. Around this time, the attic space probably became family bedrooms.

It seems that Alfred was literally a cutting-edge farmer in the country. The December 3, 1894 issue of the *Baltimore Sun* featured an article detailing his de-horning of a herd of fifty-five cattle, noting that an "operation on such an extensive scale was never before attempted in Howard County."

Alfred and Emma remained the lord and lady of the manor until 1914, when their newly married son James and his wife, Marian Ellis Brian, came into possession of the property. The newlyweds moved in with the elder Thomases, who soon welcomed two granddaughters, one in 1916 and the other in 1919.

The 1920 U.S. Census shows the extended Thomas family living at Avoca with three African American "lodgers," Charles and William Williams, ages twenty-three and eighteen, respectively, along with a widow, Sarah Scott, forty-four.

The property remained in the hands of the Thomas family until 1954, when it was sold off in parcels by one of the Thomas granddaughters. That year, Paul T. and Evelyn McHenry purchased a 25-acre parcel and later subdivided it into smaller lots. On June 27, 1959, Edward and Virginia Bethard purchased the 5.37-acre lot along with the house and numerous outbuildings.

After Virginia died in 2000, the property came into the hands of the Brethards' daughter Beatrice "Bebe" Brethard and her husband, Thomas Breen. After Bebe passed away in 2009, Thomas remained at the home. In 2016, Historic Ellicott City Inc. transformed Avoca into its annual Decorator Show House to raise funds to preserve and improve properties in and around the town's historic district.

On December 29, 2017, Thomas Breen followed his beloved wife to the grave. His estate sold Avoca for $760,000 on October 17, 2019, to Avoca LLC, which has plans to develop the property and hopefully preserve the manor house—and the spirit who still dwells within its walls.

# The Haunting

Most owners of haunted houses discover their ghosts gradually. They hear unexplained knockings or footsteps. They're puzzled when personal items disappear, only to be discovered in some odd place later. They might sense a presence or feel an unexpected chill. Or they might see someone who seems as alive and real as they are but find out that the person died long ago.

Few if any ghostly presences are announced by a knock on the front door, as was the case with the infamous spirit that roams the halls of Avoca.

The knock came in 1965, just three weeks after Edward and Virginia Bethard moved into the house, which they called the Vineyards. As the story goes, Virginia answered the door to find a wizened old man who told her he was very familiar with the property and offered to tell her what he knew about the grounds and the house.

As they walked around the yard, he pointed out various notable specimens of plants and trees, then he stopped and asked her a question.

"Have you met Emily Thomas yet?" he inquired.

Assuming she might be a neighbor, Virginia answered that, no, she hadn't.

Raising an eyebrow, the old man proceeded to tell her that she and her family were not alone in their new old house. The spirit of a woman would make herself known to them in due time.

She listened to the old man with polite interest but dismissed his revelation as a harmless ghost story she could entertain friends with on some dark and stormy night. After he left, she busied herself with unpacking and almost forgot about it, until one week later.

The Bethards were in the kitchen when they heard it: slow, even footsteps descending the narrow back steps that led from the old servants' quarters. When the sound of the footsteps stopped at the bottom of the staircase, they watched wide-eyed as the doorknob jiggled and turned several times. When they opened the door, no one was there.

Emily had just introduced herself to the new owners of her beloved home.

Over the years, the Bethards made peace with the ghost that they described as making herself known in "gentle and unfrightening" ways. Emily was said to be very social, with a fondness for parties. She had a habit of "following" family members around the house until they shooed her away.

It's said that she's shown herself in the house only twice and only to visitors. The first was to a party guest who asked Mrs. Bethard about the identity of "the elderly lady in the long gray dress in the kitchen." When they both went back to check, Emily had disappeared.

Visitors found the second appearance and subsequent manifestations much more disturbing. A visitor who one night stayed over with his cousin in what had been made into a second-floor apartment above the kitchen was awakened the next morning by the sound of floorboards creaking to the rhythm of a rocking chair. When he opened his sleep-bleary eyes, Emily was there in her dark-gray dress, rocking for a few moments until she faded away.

A house sitter, too, was unnerved by Emily's presence. He reported that after heading to his bedroom on the second floor, the family's two Great Danes immediately ran out of the room. Once in bed, he felt a presence that rattled him so much that he jumped out of bed to leave the room. Before he could get to the door, the lights suddenly went on and the radio started playing. That was enough for him. When Virginia came home, she found him cowering under a blanket on the living-room sofa.

Other indications that the ghost is around have been the sounds of ethereally beautiful music coming from an unseen organ in the living room, as well as the sudden, unexplained tinkling notes of a tune emanating from a child's long-broken windup bear.

A final account details how the spirit made itself known to a tenant hanging pictures in the apartment. It frightened him so badly that he fell off a ladder and swore at the spirit like a sailor. The next night, he came home to find the pictures he had hung the day before smashed to bits on the floor in the middle of the room.

A friend of Bebe's recounted a séance they had in the front parlor. "Some crazy things happened, and I went home and told my Mom, who showed me Bible verses and telling me not to participate again. I still get cold chills thinking about it. The candle fire got bright and high and then it went out. There was a breeze in the room. I think they had an Ouija board that went crazy. We all freaked out, laughing and running, Oh, never again!"

So, did an Emily Thomas ever really live at Avoca? And if so, who was she?

The unknown old man who knocked at Avoca's door told Mrs. Bethard that Emily Thomas was an old "maiden" lady who had lived at the house all her life.

After sifting back through the history of those who lived—and died—at the house, the author determined that the truth may be much stranger and far more tragic than the elderly gentleman's tale.

The first piece of evidence is that there really was an Emily Thomas.

She was one of the two daughters of James and Marian Thomas. Her full name was Marian Emily Thomas, and she was born at Avoca in 1916. Her younger sister, Martha, was born there in 1919.

The family moved into the home with their grandparents, Alfred and Emma, in 1914, shortly after James Clark and Marian had gotten married.

Alfred continued farming with the help of his son, who had become an attorney. The multigenerational family enjoyed just six years of happiness, sharing the joy of the girls' births and family activities before the first tragedies struck.

As in 1844, when the Pues lost two daughters, 1922 was a year that brought double deaths at Avoca. On June 10, the grandfather Alfred Thomas died at the family home "from the infirmities of old age" at age eighty. Just six months later, his forty-four-year-old son James followed him to St. John's Cemetery on December 23 after a yearlong illness.

The widowed mother-in-law and daughter-in-law soldiered on, bound together by a grief that would soon deepen.

A short eight months later, on September 28, 1923, the Angel of Death once again descended on Avoca. It bypassed Emma and Marian and, instead, spirited away three-year-old Martha on the wings of diphtheria. The despair of losing three of the most important people in their lives must have taken a tremendous toll on the two women.

In the end, the sorrow may have been just too much to bear. Emma departed this life at Avoca on December 7, 1927. Perhaps crushed by overwhelming sadness, her daughter-in-law Marian followed her loved ones to a burial plot at St. John's Cemetery two years later on a cold winter's day, February 23, 1929. She was only forty-six.

The new mistress of Avoca was the newly orphaned twelve-year-old Marian Emily Thomas—a girl who had lost everyone she'd ever loved in the space of just seven years.

What was she going to do? Stay alone at the three-hundred-acre farm? Where was she going to go?

Her aunt, who lived in Roland Park, took her in. But she returned to her childhood home almost every weekend, taking the streetcar into Ellicott City to enjoy the farm and ride her horse.

On a trip to attend a wedding in Portland, Maine, she met and eventually married Lester Cleveland Wilbur Jr. The family settled in at Avoca and had two daughters, Marian "Peggy" Thomas in 1939 and Georgia in 1940.

Unfortunately, the marriage didn't last. After her divorce, Marian Emily met and married Ervin Getman McCloskey in 1943. She and McCloskey, a fertilizer industry executive nearly thirty years her senior, continued to enjoy the pleasures of farm life at Avoca. They welcomed a son, Thomas Getman McCloskey, in 1944.

The family had planned to move to South Carolina in 1953, but before they could, Ervin passed away on June 6 at the age of sixty-six. After his death, Emily and her children left Avoca and moved south for a little over a year.

On October 5, 1954, seventy-six years after her grandfather and grandmother bought Avoca, Marian Emily Thomas McCloskey sold the family home and land and moved to the warmth of Florida to raise her children.

The little girl who was born at Avoca and endured so much in life died in DeLeon, Florida, on December 20, 1987, at the age of seventy-one—which means that Emily Thomas was still very much alive when the ghost who bore her name first began appearing at the Bethard home in the 1960s.

Without a paranormal investigation, the true identity of the spectral old lady in the long gray dress that haunts the halls of the old granite mansion may never be known for certain.

However, one can speculate.

Emily's mother died at Avoca in 1927 at the age of forty-six, filled with great sadness at the time of her passing, certainly, but far too young to appear as an elderly woman in antique garb.

More likely, the spirit that appears in the small rooms above the kitchen is actually that of Emma Ward Clark Thomas, a woman who was born in 1847 and lived at Avoca for nearly fifty years. She died at the age of eighty, broken-hearted after the successive deaths of her husband, son and three-year-old granddaughter.

And indeed, according to the real Emily's daughter, that's who the Thomas family always believed to be the ghost.

One can easily imagine the old woman rocking a very sick little girl to sleep up in the servants' quarters night after night; creeping down the back steps to bring up a bottle of warm milk to comfort her; and crying soft tears onto the girl's fevered face before the child's spirit fluttered out of her arms to join her father and grandfather in the world beyond this one.

Whatever her name, the energy and sorrow of the elderly woman in the long gray dress wanted to remain behind to stay with any of the other spirits that may haunt Avoca.

# 2

# BELMONT MANOR

## ELKRIDGE

*An early-1700s manor house is home to a host of ghosts,*
*including the tormented soul of a madman murderer.*

Set a long way back from the road with a curving drive that offers visitors a welcoming view of what Paul Wilstach in his 1931 *Tidewater Maryland* book described as "an inviting survivor of the past, where nearly all else is the product of the present…is a long brick mansion of center house, curtain, and two-story wings, and is called Belmont." Located at 6555 Belmont Woods Road, the nearly three-hundred-year-old house ranks among the oldest surviving structures in Howard County.

Home to seven generations of the Dorsey family before it passed into commercial and public hands, the gracious building and grounds went on to become a historical, cultural and environmental center. Today, Belmont Manor stands as a testament to its romantic beginnings and its connection to Howard County's agricultural, industrial and political history.

Tales of the lives and deaths of the hardworking men and headstrong women as well as a legion of friendly, frustrated and anguished spirits continue to capture the imagination of history buffs and visitors alike.

# THE HISTORY

What today is known as Belmont Manor stands on a 1,368-acre land grant called "Moore's Morning Choice" that was first surveyed and patented in 1695 by Dr. Mordecai Moore. A founder of the Friends Society of Maryland and a land speculator, Moore was married to the second wife and widow of Colonel William Burgess of Londontown.

In 1732, Caleb Dorsey Sr. of Annapolis and Hockley-in-the Hole on the Severn River and his wife, Elinor Warfield, purchased the land. The couple had a total of thirteen children, including Caleb Jr., who, along with his brother Edward, would make his fortune operating several iron forges along tributaries that lead to the Patapsco.

In addition to being a budding iron magnate, Caleb Jr. was an avid fox hunter. It's said that once while tracking a rare gray fox, his hunt took him on to the property of the Hill family in West River. In the course of finishing his hunt, he met the Hills' teenage daughter Priscilla Embry Hill. They struck up a friendship that quickly blossomed into romance.

On February 10, 1735, twenty-five-year-old Caleb Jr. married seventeen-year-old Priscilla. Caleb Sr. gave "Moore's Morning Choice" to the smitten young couple as a wedding gift. A little more than a year after they were married, in March 1736, they welcomed their first son, Henry Hill Dorsey, and began dreaming of the home they would build for their family.

In 1738, the same year Priscilla's father, Henry Applewhite Hill, died, the Dorseys began building their colonial Georgian house. It was often referred to as the home of "the rich Iron Merchant of Elkridge." The original center part of the house was a fifty-foot-wide structure made of brick said to have been brought over from England on Caleb Jr.'s own ship. On either side of the front door, they installed two carved plaques that read "CPD 1738"—their initials and the date the house was built.

Said to be quite superstitious, Dorsey also bolted huge iron crosses onto his doors. Known as "witches crosses," they were part of a New England tradition that may be rooted in the English practice of putting "witches marks" on buildings. These were usually etched onto stone or woodwork near a home's entrance points, including doorways, windows and fireplaces, to protect inhabitants and visitors from witches and evil spirits.

As an iron merchant, Caleb's choice of metal was a natural one. However, whether Dorsey knew it or not, in folklore, cold iron is supposed to protect against witches, fairies and evil spirits, who are unable to cross it. Iron was used in classical times to ward off evil spirits that caused illness and bad

Belmont's circular drive welcomes visitors—and a murder victim—to its front door. *Maryland Historical Trust.*

luck and was a special protection for vulnerable women in childbirth and small children. Iron ore or cast iron from the British Isles and Europe were brought over to the colonies and laid across the threshold or inset into the main doorframe to prevent malevolent beings from entering the home.

After the house was finished, Caleb and Priscilla quickly began filling up their new home with children. Their son Henry Hill was born in 1726 and daughter Rebecca in 1839, followed by son Samuel in 1741. Then came daughters Mary Pue in 1744, Milcah in 1747, Eleanor in 1749, Margaret Peggy Hill in 1752 and Priscilla on June 26, 1754.

Tragically, the Angel of Death came for little Priscilla at the age of two in 1756. She was buried in the family cemetery at the rear of the house. Dorsey's last son, Edward Hill, was born two years later. In 1762, the couple was blessed by the birth of their last daughter, whom they named Priscilla, after her mother and the daughter they had lost earlier.

The first Priscilla wasn't the last of the Dorsey children to precede their father in death. On March 7, 1772, just four years after he married Elizabeth Goodwin, Henry Hill Dorsey crossed over into eternity. Only thirty-six years old, Dorsey's eldest son was buried in Mount Olivet Cemetery in Baltimore.

On June 28, 1772, a little more than three months after his son's death, Caleb Jr. also departed this life. Although he had no formal education and was said to have owned few books, thanks to his father's gift of land and income from farming, his forges and foundries, Caleb Jr. was immensely wealthy. At the time of his death, he owned three thousand acres, ninety-four enslaved people, 466 head of livestock and personal belongings valued at £8,000. In accordance with a request in his will, which was executed just a week after Henry's death, no sermon was preached at his burial.

Dorsey's son Edward, a strong-fisted, big-hearted man who became known as "Iron Head Ned," inherited the property. His brother Samuel helped him maintain it until his death in 1777. Priscilla, Caleb Jr.'s widow, lived there until she joined her husband in the cemetery in 1782.

Edward preserved the estate and expanded it to 3,245 acres. He increased the number of enslaved people to 114 and kept the family's forges at Elk Ridge and Curtis Creek running until tax problems forced their closure in 1783. In 1786, he married his cousin Elizabeth. They had three daughters, Mary in 1787, Priscilla in 1789 and Caroline in 1791. Their son Hammond came along in 1793. Just six years later, in 1799, Edward breathed his last in his Belmont bedroom. Elizabeth followed him to the grave in 1802.

In 1805, Dorsey's headstrong daughter Priscilla eloped with Alexander Contee Hanson Jr. since the guardians she was living with in Baltimore would not give their consent. On their way to Annapolis to get married, a wheel pin on their carriage broke. Fortunately, the groom had a spare on board to fix it, otherwise the wedding would have likely been postponed.

As the grandson of a member of the Continental Congress, a U.S. congressman and a senator representing Maryland, Hanson must have seemed like a great catch. Their son Alexander Contee was born in 1807, followed by Edward Pickering in 1809. Daughter Mary Rebecca came along in 1811, James Lingan in 1813 and then Caroline in 1814.

In 1815, when the Dorsey estate was portioned, Priscilla received the house along with a substantial amount of land. She christened it Belmont. It's said that "the children of Priscilla Dorsey and Alexander Contee Hanson were many but only one lived to maturity," Charles Grosvener, who was born in 1816. Another child, Mary Jane, was born in 1818. Evidently, she died young, as her name disappears from the records and there is no documentation of a marriage or children.

As busy as Priscilla was birthing doomed babies and running Belmont, Alexander was even busier—and to no good end. In addition to serving in

Congress as a U.S. representative (1811–13), he also served as a senator (1818–19). What got him into trouble was his role as the founder of the extremist, pro-British newspaper the *Federal Republican*. At the time, Hanson's views were so unpopular that during the War of 1812 a mob attacked the offices of the newspaper. He was arrested and taken to jail, where the mob found him again, beat him and left him for dead. It seems he really never recovered from his injuries and passed into the next world in 1819 at the age of just thirty-three.

As promising as his future had seemed when Priscilla married him, when Hanson left this mortal world, he left very little behind. His political and publishing activities had drained his savings as well as the inheritance left to his wife. Priscilla tried as hard as she could to keep Belmont going, but the financial burden was too great. In the 1830s, she began selling off parcels of the land. It got so bad that, in 1839, the great-great-granddaughter of Caleb Dorsey Sr. mortgaged Belmont for $1,500.

To compound her misery, her son Charles was a horse-racing and gambling addict. Realizing that his problems could cost the family the farm, Priscilla drew up a will before her death in 1849 that stated that if Charles ever put the estate in jeopardy, it would be transferred to his wife, Anna "Annie" Maria Worthington, and her family.

Like most couples of that time, Charles and Anna Maria had a large family. Various records show they had up to six sons (Alexander Contee Jr., Charles Edward "Ned," Murray, Samuel Contee, Grosvenor and Christopher) and up to seven daughters (Priscilla, Mary, Annie Marie "Nannie," twins Alice Howard and Bessie Lee, as well as Elizabeth and Florence C.) As was not uncommon in that era, a number of them died young. Alexander Contee died in 1857 at the age of seventeen. The couple's one-year-old twins, Alice and Bessie, both died in 1865. The children's mother, Annie Maria, died in 1873.

In 1875, Priscilla Hanson's worst nightmare became a reality.

With no money to pay bills and Belmont now reduced to six hundred acres, the property went to a sheriff's auction, where it sold for twenty-five dollars. Fortunately, because of Priscilla's will, the auction was contested, and the property came back to Charles's and Anna Marie's children in 1879.

Nearly as superstitious as Caleb Dorsey Jr., Charles believed that if he did any work on the Belmont family cemetery, it would cause him to go to an early grave. So, he neglected the burial ground, and it fell into ruin. The house, too, descended into disrepair after his wife died. On October 17, 1880, despite his best efforts to outrun the Grim Reaper, he died at the age of sixty-four. Charles Grosvenor Hanson was buried in the brambles of the purposely unkempt grounds of the Belmont Manor Cemetery.

After that, the property remained in the hands of the Hanson family. Anna Maria and Charles's youngest surviving daughters, twenty-two-year-old Annie Maria (Nannie) and twenty-year-old Florence C., stayed on at Belmont. Their siblings all moved away.

It seems the sisters never married. An account from 1905 recalls that Miss Nannie and Miss Florence "made preserves and pickles to sell which they stored in the ballroom." The 1910 U.S. Census shows them living on the property with African American servants Daniel and Alverta Lewis.

In 1917, Nannie sold the property to her cousin Mary Bowdoin Bruce, a seventh-generation descendant of Caleb Jr. and Priscilla Dorsey. Suddenly, Belmont's fortunes were looking up. Mary's husband Howard Bruce was the vice-president and general manager of Bartlett Hayward Company, and he became even more successful during World War I. For his exemplary service during the war effort, Bruce received the Distinguished Service Award, the highest award bestowed on a civilian, and was recognized for his work as director of material for armed services.

The couple set about returning the home and property to its former glory. There was a lot to restore. Over the centuries, the manor house had grown to three times its original size and now boasted twenty-seven rooms.

In addition to the manor house, the grounds and barns were overhauled as well to accommodate the equine royalty of Howard's Thoroughbred horse, Billy Barton. Handsome and hot-blooded, the horse took top honors at the Maryland Hunt Club in 1926 and, two years later, finished second in the Grand National Steeplechase in Aintree, England. When Billy Barton finally galloped off into the sunset in 1951, he was buried in a very unusual way. The horse was interred near the barn, standing upright in full tack with saddle and bridle on, eternally ready to be off to the races. When Billy Barton's stablemate Jay Jay passed away in 1963, he was buried alongside his longtime equine friend.

In 1961, Howard Bruce passed away. His widow went to live in Baltimore, and Belmont came into the possession of Howard Bruce's cousin David K.E. Bruce, former ambassador to France, Germany and Great Britain. Since David already owned an old family estate in Virginia, Bruce sold Belmont to the Smithsonian Institution in 1964 for $500,000.

The Smithsonian converted Belmont into a conference center, where generals, vice presidents, astronauts and many other notables came to meet on important national matters. Unfortunately, maintaining the property was extraordinarily expensive.

In 1983, the Smithsonian sold the house and outbuildings along with eighty-five acres of land to the American Chemical Society, which continued to use it as a meeting venue. Twenty one-years later, the society sold it to Howard County Community college for $5.2 million, partially covered by a $2.6 million loan from the Howard County government.

By 2010, the burden of maintaining the property once again became too heavy for the owners to bear. On June 21, 2012, Howard County purchased Belmont from the college in exchange for $89,000 in cash and forgiving the $2.6 million debt. The county government sold thirteen acres of the land to developers, leaving sixty-eight acres of the original property, enough to preserve its near-pristine colonial-era "view-scape."

Howard County opened Belmont Manor and Historic Park to the public in April 2015. It is now operated by the county's Department of Recreation and Parks and welcomes visitors for weddings, private events and environmental education programs—and incredibly well-attended ghost tours. It seems the lure of Belmont's myriad spirits is just as strong as its history and natural beauty.

# THE HAUNTING

*Sometimes on dark and windy nights, in the old house, you hear the Belmont ghost. At least once a winter, does it come. Perhaps you are sitting before the open fireplace in which* [a visitor] *delighted. You hear the wind lonesomely without, then suddenly there is the sound of horses' hooves and the jangling of harnesses; many horses evidently, and the harness and wheels seem to creak and rumble more heavily than harness and wheels of nowadays.*

*You start for the door, but you hear the rustle of other footsteps ahead of you on the same errand, though you see no one. The door opens and there is the scraping of feet as people come in. You are now standing up in alarm.*

*"What is it?" she asks.*

*But there is only a long-drawn-out sigh. This then is the sound of some of the forefathers coming home from Annapolis in coach and six. You hear the sounds of wheels driving away around the house toward the stables, the creak of harnesses, and the clattering of hooves. The rest is silence. The woman is heard no more. This is the Belmont ghost.*

*—a combined account of Daniel De Lee Dorsey, "The Dorsey Family" (1951), and* Colonial Mansions of Maryland and Delaware, *by John Martin Hammond.*

"The" Belmont ghost? More like one of a multitude of ghosts that glide through the formal rooms, busy themselves in the servants' quarters and peek out of its ancient windows.

Most everyone interested in history and the supernatural knows that Elliott City has a well-deserved reputation as the most haunted town in Maryland. But few are aware of the supernatural phenomena and the legions of ghosts that haunt the grand parlors, private bedrooms and grounds of Belmont Manor. Home to nearly three centuries of history, seven generations of Dorseys and the final resting place of dozens of its former inhabitants, the property has been the site of ghostly encounters since its earliest days.

According to paranormal investigator Rob Gutrow of Inspired Ghost Tracking, who has had access to Belmont since it came into the hands of Howard County Recreation and Parks and conducts regular ghost tours, there are five to six intelligent hauntings at Belmont, with the rest being residual hauntings.

What's the difference?

Intelligent hauntings are those in which the spirit interacts or communicates with the living. They've chosen to stay here because they feel a connection with a place, a person or a traumatic experience that they don't want to or can't let go of. Some might want to communicate a message from the other side, are leery of proceeding into the unknown or are fearful of punishment in the afterlife. Others may simply not realize that they are dead.

Signs of an intelligent haunting include doors opening and closing; odd sounds; objects being hidden or moved; a creepy, goose-bumps feeling; and the disturbance of electrical devices, like lights, TVs or radios turning on and off.

Residual hauntings are much more common. They are best described as when the ghost of a person, animal or event is witnessed doing the same thing over and over again. It's believed that the residual energy of an emotionally charged event can leave an imprint or what can be described as a "photograph in time" that may be triggered by the energy of a living person.

Based on those criteria, the ghostly "coach and six" manifestation at Belmont is likely a residual haunting. Others that interact with investigators, visitors and employees at the manor clearly qualify as intelligent hauntings.

Perhaps the most famous of Belmont's ghosts is the wraith of a beautiful six-year-old child known as Amanda. She was supposedly the daughter of a wealthy businessman and related to someone who lived at the house in the 1700s. Conversations with the spirit have indicated that she likely died of the flu or pneumonia. With her curly blond hair tucked back in a ponytail and her flowing blue nightgown, those who have seen the materialized spirit of Amanda say she looks like a doll or Alice in Wonderland.

She has appeared to workmen and other men who may resemble her father. Those who have seen her describe the spirit child happily running through the halls on the first floor or wandering through bedrooms upstairs. Amanda is said to love the sound of the piano downstairs. She occasionally makes her presence known by tugging on visitors' clothes.

Nearly as notorious as Amanda is the ghost of Andrew Lyons, also known as the "grumpy man." He was supposedly a merchant who may have run barges on the Patapsco or brought lumber from western Maryland to Belmont. He's described by those who've seen him as having big hands, smoking a pipe and sporting mutton-chop sideburns that were the fashion in the late 1800s. It's said that while delivering a load of timber to Belmont to build a barn, he keeled over of a massive heart attack. He was brought up to the right front-side bedroom, where he died.

Who might he be?

A cursory look at the 1870 U.S. Census shows Andrew Lyons as a laborer born in 1852. At the time, he was living in Baltimore's Seventeenth Ward, which encompasses South Baltimore, Riverside and Locust Point along the Patapsco River. Present-day staff at Belmont report that Mr. Lyons doesn't like fish and makes his displeasure known when they serve it.

Perhaps because he died at a relatively young age and supposedly left behind a wife and a daughter, he is an "earthbound" spirit who may eternally be in foul spirits because he wasn't able to say goodbye to his family. He may not know how to cross over or may not want to. And so, this surly specter remains at Belmont, fuming about his lost family, a pipe that won't light and the smell of an occasional fish dish wafting up to his room.

Not all of the ghosts of Belmont are from the distant past. At least one is of more recent vintage. He is said to be a disgruntled U.S. general who met in secret with other military and government officials to plan the first Gulf War in 1990. The haunting takes place in a room down a long hall along the right side of the building.

The manifestation of his spirit is the sound of a cane or chairs scraping on the floor. Visitors also feel chest pain and light-headedness when in the room. People sensitive to spirits describe him as an angry and gruff man who has something that he wants to get off his chest. Evidently, the decisions he played a part in haunted him and drew him back to Belmont after he died, because, "It wasn't the right thing to do."

Other specters include an older, white-haired woman who appears in the kitchen and dining areas, where plates and silverware are arranged by unseen hands and where olives have been thrown across the room. Upstairs is another angry female spirit who "really hates people." A much more pleasant spirit is the ghost of a gentleman in the bar area who seems to be enjoying an eternal beer.

While most all of the ghosts at Belmont seem to have passed into some form of the afterlife as innocent as the day they were born, one did not.

The apparition of a man who looks to be in his thirties or forties dressed in riding pants with white breeches and boots has been seen staring out the window of the piano room of the mansion. A medium who contacted the spirit said that the ghost was involved in a murder just outside the front door—maybe as the victim, perhaps as the murderer himself. She said that, for some reason, the ghost couldn't hear or was deaf. During her contact with the spirit, she said she heard a loud sound that might have been a gunshot.

The spirit calls back to a true event? Or a fanciful imagining?

Sadly, it is the former. A recently discovered news item in the May 17, 1883 edition of the *Baltimore Sun* proves that the murder actually happened and gives clues as to who this tragic Belmont ghost might be.

It seems that just before noon on May 16, 1883, Charles Ridgely White, a fifty-nine-year-old neighbor, made his way to Belmont from his farm, Argyle, which was located a mile above Ilchester. He had come to meet thirty-five-year-old Charles Edward "Ned" Hanson, the son of Charles Grosvenor Hanson, to get some seed corn.

Hanson was not there at the time but returned before White left. Hanson asked his sister who had come to the house. When she told him, he nonchalantly walked to the dining room, picked up a bread knife from the sideboard and walked out to where White was waiting to start for home.

When he got to within ten feet of White, Hanson suddenly pulled out a revolver. Without saying a single word, he shot White three times in the head. He then threw himself on White's soon-to-be lifeless body and used the bread knife to slash a four-inch gash across his throat, partially severing his windpipe.

Hanson then calmly went back inside Belmont, washed the blood off the knife and went up to his room to wait for his brothers John and Grosvenor to get back from Baltimore. When they arrived, Edward was raving and gave them a variety of incoherent reasons for the shooting.

He told them that when their mother was dying, her last wish was that he should kill Charles White, because he had supposedly "killed" his sister Mary (who had died of consumption in 1863). That claim aside, the death-bed wish was patently false, since Hanson was not present at his mother's death. Edward also accused White of "flashing his eyes"—a habit of rather violently blinking his eyes that Hanson himself had—in order to taunt him.

Justice was swift. At 4:00 p.m. that very day, Justice J.N. Gordon impaneled a jury of inquest at Belmont, where the murder victim's dead body remained. White's still-warm corpse was examined by Drs. H. Tongue and E.W. Eareckson of Elkridge Landing. Their report read as follows:

> *One ball passed through the right cheek below the angle of the jawbone, passing downward and backward, entering some of the bones of the shoulder. A second which passed through Mr. White's hand entered the back of the neck and produced a superficial wound. The ball was extracted. The third entered the left temple an inch back of the eye, piercing entirely through the brain. The throat was cut as already described.*

At the conclusion of the testimony by the doctors and witnesses, the jury rendered a verdict: Hanson had killed White and was insane at the time of the murder. His brothers took him to the Ellicott City Jail.

The next day, Hanson's story changed. He claimed that he had acted in self-defense, saying that the spirit of his dead sister had appeared to warn him that White was out to get him and would shoot him on sight. When he was questioned on other subjects, Hanson spoke clearly and quietly. But the moment the shooting was mentioned, his eyes "snapped," and his talk became wild and disconnected. Hanson's brothers said he'd shown signs of mental illness after he came back from California and later suffered sunstroke, which they thought worsened it.

On May 19, Hanson's murder victim, Charles Ridgely White, was taken to be buried at St. John's Cemetery. A newspaper article reported, "It was a long, silent dusty drive and would have almost been unendurable had not the fragrancy of the wild honeysuckle and the varying tints of the grass and trees given a refreshing yet quiet and beautiful charm to the scene."

The next month, on June 11, 1883, a special session of the Howard County Court was convened to determine the mental condition of Charles Edward Hanson. After hearing testimony about his recent history of unrestrained paranoia and bouts of unhinged anger, the jury retired to render a decision. Within minutes, they came back with a verdict: "Adjudged Insane and

Committed to an Asylum." As punishment, Hanson was committed to the Maryland Hospital for the Insane.

Tragically insanity seemed to run in the Hanson family.

Just a few years later but prior to 1900, Charles's eldest sister, Priscilla, was also committed to the Maryland Hospital for the Insane. Perhaps mental illness was heredity, or maybe the horror of the murder and her brother's conviction drove Hanson's spinster sister out of her mind. Whatever the cause, both she and Charles remained at various iterations of the state facility until they died. Priscilla passed away there on April 16, 1925, at the age of seventy-eight. Her brother, the murderer, died at Spring Grove State Hospital as well in 1931 at the age of eighty-eight.

Both brother's and sister's bodies—and evidently their spirits—returned to Belmont Manor, where their mortal remains were buried in the family graveyard. Their monuments along with many others stand alongside generations of other family members' headstones and as many as seventy-three unmarked graves.

Today, the ghost of madman murderer Charles Edward Hanson keeps an eternal eye out for unlucky visitors from the window of the piano room, while the wraith of his insane older sister Priscilla keeps company with the host of friendly, fierce and forlorn spirits that haunt the grand halls at Belmont Manor.

# 3

# HILL HOUSE

## ELLICOTT CITY

*Once ruined, now restored, a judge's former home harbors
the ghost of the owner who loved it most.*

Perched on a rise just above the Judge's Bench restaurant and bar on Main Street stands this quaint hewn-granite home at 8505 Hill Street. Surrounded by carefully crafted stone terraces and lovely landscaping, the charming dwelling is known as Hill House. Perhaps because of its unclear origins and a history pockmarked by years of neglect, there is little official documentation of the building's beginnings.

That being said, the memories of the house, its former inhabitants and the ghosts they left behind are not unhappy ones. One spirit, in particular, keeps eternal watch and occasionally extends a welcoming hand to those who love the house as much as they did.

## THE HISTORY

Built in the Quaker-inspired Federal style that is the hallmark of early Ellicott City buildings, Hill House stands on what was originally part of the Mount Misery land grant patented to Thomas, Elias and William Brown in the 1700s.

No accounts of exactly who built the structure have been found, but a previous owner dates the building to 1824, based on artifacts found at the home. The tax records say it was built in 1838. In any case, by the mid-1800s, there was a house on the property, because, on June 1, 1866, Ernest Luther Timanus purchased the home from the executors of the estates of Richard B. Brown and Margery B. Anderson for $1,400. The property was officially identified as Lots 19, 20 and 21 on the plat of "Elias Brown and others."

Married to Mary Frances George, Luther was a member of the well-known Timanus family in Randallstown. He served as justice of the peace later as a judge of the Orphan's Court for Baltimore County, eventually becoming chief justice. The Timanuses may have bought Hill House as an investment; just a year earlier, they had purchased Powhatan, the Timanus family's old homestead in Baltimore County.

Luther was the son of Jacob Timanus Jr. and Margaret Mansfield, Jacob's second wife. His first wife was Jane McCullough, who died in 1823. Among the children from that first marriage was a daughter, Louisa, a half-sister to Luther. Born in 1818 into this prominent family, Louisa was educated at the then newly opened Patapsco Female Institute in Ellicott City. She would eventually become the mistress of Hill House.

Despite her pedigree and education, it seems that Louisa didn't marry terribly well. According to the 1850 U.S. Census, she was living in Ellicott City with her husband, Isaac Sullivan Strawbridge, a tailor at a dress shop at the time. The Strawbridges had two daughters. Margaret Ann was born in 1842, and Anna Mariah in 1852. Like their mother, both girls attended the Patapsco Female Institute.

The 1860 U.S. Census shows Isaac's and Louisa's occupations as "Keeping a Boarding House" and not owning any real estate. At the time, eighteen-year-old Margaret was living with them and was employed as a teacher. They had an African American house servant, Cynthia Budd, and four boarders, including Oliver A. Prescott, a "PE clergyman" from Connecticut.

On July 2, 1876, the Strawbridge family's fortunes improved considerably. Louisa's half-brother Luther and his wife sold Hill House and the three lots to his sister. After years of renting, the Strawbridges finally had a home of their own.

In April 1877, the Strawbridges' daughter Margaret Ann married Charles F. Bierly, a boot- and shoemaker. Around that time, Louisa and Isaac, who were getting up in years, passed on ownership of Hill House and its property to their daughters. They remained in their quaint stone home. Unfortunately, whatever happiness they had in their first few years was short-lived.

Front entrance and stone terraces leading up to the home's first floor, 2020. *Steve Freeman*.

The first known death at Hill House came in 1879, when Isaac Sullivan Strawbridge, a veteran of the Mexican War and commissary sergeant in Colonel John Eager Howard's Voltigeurs, departed this life at the age of sixty-five.

Devastated by the loss of her husband, Louisa's sorrow was likely eased by the joy of the birth of her first grandchild, Frank Bierly, in 1880, and then by the marriage of her daughter Anna Mariah to a bank bookkeeper, John M. Collier, in 1881. That joy was compounded many times over by the rapid-fire births of her grandchildren John, Louis, William, Robert and Oswald Collier, who was born in 1893.

On November 14, 1889, the Angel of Death carried Louisa off to her eternal rest. The seventy-eight-year-old "aged lady" did not die at Hill House, but at the home of her daughter Margaret Ann and son-in-law Charles Bierly. Her obituary noted that she was a fifty-year resident of Ellicott City and a sixty-five-year member of "the Methodist Episcopal Church," now Emory United Methodist Church. Both Louisa and Isaac were buried at Mount Olive Cemetery in Randallstown, where the Bierlys would eventually join them. Their family headstone is inscribed with a phrase from Psalm 127:2 "He giveth His beloved sleep."

In 1905, Charles Bierly died and Margaret Ann bought out her sister Anna Mariah Collier's share of Hill House. Three years later, on September 14, 1908, she sold the property to Margaret Horner McCaffrey. Margaret and her husband, John Arthur McCafferty, a retired justice of the peace, presumably moved into the house. Presumably, because the 1910 U.S. Census shows Margaret's cousin, James Steward, a grocery clerk, and his wife, Mary, as heads of the household, with Margaret and John living there as boarders.

Death came for John McCafferty on October 5, 1923, at the age of seventy-six. His obituary noted that he was a descendant of veterans of the War of 1812 and the Revolutionary War. His funeral was held at his home, Woodlawn Hall, in Ellicott City, and he was buried at St. John's Cemetery.

Even before her husband's death, it seems that Margaret may have fallen on hard times. The 1930 U.S. Census once again shows her living with her cousin James; his wife, Mary; and their two sons, James, a railroad clerk, and John, above their grocery store on Frederick Turnpike in Ellicott City.

Records also show three liens being taken out on Hill House, one, on May 9, 1923, six months before John McCafferty's death, then two more in April and December 1932. In 1934, Margaret drew up a will, leaving Hill House to her cousin's son John Arthur Steward.

Two years later, on May 22, 1936, Margaret passed away at the age of eighty-eight after an illness of a few days. Her obituary described Mrs. McCafferty as "one of the oldest residents of Ellicott City." The Easton Sons hearse somberly carried her body to a grave beside her husband's burial spot at St. John's.

In December 1937, John Arthur Steward came into his inheritance. Around that time in 1940, he and his wife, Ann Gist Sykes Steward, were living just off College Avenue on Weaver's Court. The Stewards had three children: Mary Ann, John Arthur Jr. and James R.

This generation of Stewards probably lived at Hill House until August 6, 1954, when they sold the property to Anna Albert and Paul Willard McDonald. The McDonalds were quite wealthy and likely bought Hill House as a rental or investment property. Their primary residence was at Spring Hill, an elegant eighteenth-century manor home on Montgomery Road that the couple purchased in 1953. After Paul McDonald passed away in 1966, Anna held on to ownership of the rapidly deteriorating Hill House property for another couple of years.

On November 25, 1968, Hill House got a shot at a new life.

On that day, Paul's widow, along with Herbert R. and Dr. Ann G. Steinmann from New York City, sold the property to Diane Gail Schulte for $4,000. The unbelievably low purchase price was well warranted. By all accounts, Hill House had pretty much fallen into an uninhabitable ruin that was on the verge of being condemned.

In a 1971 article in the *Baltimore Sun*, Schulte recalled the husk of the house she had purchased.

> *I had to force my way through the jungle of trash, vines, and tree roots that had penetrated the stone walls and into the ground floor. The house was just a shell. I could see sky through a big hole in the roof. A November rain was pouring through the three upper floors down to where I stood amid dirt and debris beneath a rotted log floor.… There was no heating, plumbing, or electricity. The only occupants for 25 years or more were rats.*

A recent graduate of George Washington University, a part-time realtor and a second-year student at the University of Maryland Law School, the young woman didn't have a lot of spare time or money. Her father helped her out financially with the renovations, but she did the lion's share of the physical labor.

It was a massive undertaking, but she persevered. In addition to studying torts and court opinions, Schulte threw herself into learning how to repoint stone and design a workable heating and cooling system. Friends and family members pitched in to help. She scavenged salvaged materials, including bricks from the courtyard of a West Franklin Street church that was being demolished to pave the first-floor dining room. Handsome stone fireplaces

Hill House teetering on the precipice of ruin, November 1968. *Diane Schulte.*

were revealed and restored. Federal-era paneling was refinished. She created an inviting landscape and terraces using huge cobblestones retrieved from a septic tank in the front yard.

Schulte filled her historic home with beautiful period antiques, rugs and other furnishings. The ground floor houses the kitchen, dining room and utility room. The second floor features a reception room and living room. The third floor is devoted to the master suite, while she opened up the fourth floor to create an airy office with views of Ellicott City. The result of her extensive restoration was so much of a showplace that it was a featured residence on the 1971 Maryland Home and Garden Pilgrimage tour.

After twelve years of enjoying the house and pursuing a stellar career that included serving as a law clerk to the Honorable James R. Miller, U.S. District Court; Assistant State's Attorney of Baltimore City; Assistant County Solicitor of Howard County; and Chief Counsel; and becoming Howard County's first female judge for the District Court of Maryland, District 10, Schulte was ready for her next adventure.

On August 21, 1980, Schulte sold Hill House to John G. Teichmoller for $105,000. Teichmoller, who worked for the Ellicott City office of Waddell and Reed Inc., went on to marry Kathy B. Farnsworth. The couple lived at Hill House until March 30, 1995, when they sold it to Dr. Ronald Tobias Eugene Rizzolo for $248,000.

Just four years later, in 1999, Rizzolo sold the home to Patricia A. Faley for $250,000. Recently widowed, Faley had purchased the home after her husband of just one year, Boris Kachura, died of a heart attack at Union Station in 1995. She lived at Hill House for a period of time but then rented the home to tenants, including Casey Caulder, who called the cozy house home between 2014 and 2016.

On January 28, 2016, Patricia Faley opened a new chapter in the history of Hill House by selling it to Nicholas James Slater and Wenchen "Katherine" Liu Slater for $460,000. Recently married in 2014, Katherine worked as a data and marine scientist and environmental statistician, and Nicholas was employed by Pasco Battery in Annapolis. Shortly after moving in, the couple welcomed a baby boy into their family.

A house that had seen its share of death and sorrow over its two-hundred-or-so-year history was now filled with the laughter and energy of new life—a new life that is perhaps watched over by a ghostly grandmother whose fierce devotion to Hill House continues to this day.

# The Haunting

With its murky beginnings and decades of neglect, Hill House had the equivalent of a near-death experience. It was likely just months away from having its sturdy granite walls and generations of memories and life experiences from past Ellicott City residents bulldozed into oblivion.

Fortunately, it—and the spirit of a long-ago lady—survived in a house that continues to look down onto Main Street from one of the prettiest perches in town.

Although the judge who resuscitated Hill House before the last of its life was snuffed out said she never had any supernatural experiences in the house, others did. An earlier owner, a gruff skeptic, told of seeing a pen levitate and fly through the air.

The most compelling account of the ghost of Hill House comes from someone who was just passing through. The spirit seems to have reached out to Casey Caulder, a spirit-sensitive renter who forged a bond of friendship with it that neither has ever forgotten.

The first sign that there was "something" or someone in the house came just a few weeks after this new tenant moved into the charming stone home. It came in the form of the sound of a loud clap Casey heard while she was sitting alone in the second-floor living room. It seemed to be coming from the library room next to her. She jumped up to look, but no one was there.

The clapping noise came again. This time, it sounded like it was coming from outside. Again, not a soul was stirring on the terraced yard outside the house. A few moments later, Casey heard the clap again, coming from downstairs in the kitchen.

The noise was loud and distinct, but it didn't scare her—at least at first.

Caulder then started thinking that an intruder might actually be in the house. That rattled her. She thought about calling her parents or just leaving. She came back upstairs to the living room to sit and mull her options. She heard it yet again, this time on the fourth floor, where the judge's study had been.

Determined to take things into her own hands, Casey ran up and slammed shut the door to the top floor, thinking she'd trap the intruder. But, of course, there was nobody on this side of the grave to trap.

A few weeks later, the ghost made itself known again.

The young tenant was awakened from a dead sleep by the distinct sensation that someone was hovering over her, breathing directly and

Judge Schulte enjoying the rear gardens at the home she restored in the 1970s. *Diane Schulte.*

heavily into her sleeping face. Startled, she sat up in bed and decided to give the entity a talking to.

Caulder told whatever had come upon her that waking her up like that was "uncool." She assured the spirit that she knew it was there and that they could share the cozy quarters, but it must never, ever scare her like that again.

It seemed that whatever was in the house was checking her out, wondering who she was and deciding whether or not it liked her. In the end, the tenant got the sense that the spirit was indeed sorry for scaring her.

From then on, the ghostly presence was like a friendly roommate who was always there. In fact, the young woman said that whenever she entered the home, it felt like she was getting "a big hug." She got into the habit of announcing that she was home or that guests were coming to visit.

The ghost seemed to have full run of the house, although it "slept" in the room on the top floor. The tenant got a sense that the entity was an older woman of average build who wore her hair short or up in a bun. She was prim and proper, didn't cook and may have had a dog. For whatever reason, the elderly spirit was drawn to an antique wardrobe and the bathroom on the third floor. The ghost especially liked the tenant's collection of vintage compacts and a particularly beautiful crystal perfume atomizer she displayed there.

A communication breakthrough came when the lights on the third floor stopped working. After determining that the lightbulbs were in working order, the renter impatiently addressed the ghost and asked if it was doing it.

"Flicker the lights twice if the answer is yes," Casey said.

The answer came back in the affirmative.

Heartened, she asked another question: "Do you want me here?"

The ghost again flickered "yes."

Friends who came to visit were introduced to the ghost, who sometimes interacted with them via the flickering lights. The tenant always told visitors that Hill House belonged to the spirit and that they had to respect it and her.

Eventually, the day came when the young woman decided to move on. She had purchased a farmhouse and began making preparations to move out. As she was packing her things, she sensed the spirit following her from room to room. Sad to leave her unseen but always present friend, Casey asked the spirit if it could come with her to her new home or perhaps visit?

The lights flickered once.

While she was gathering her things in the third-floor bath, Casey picked up the antique perfume atomizer that she knew the ghost liked.

"Would you like to have this?" the renter inquired.

The lights flickered twice.

With that, she took the beautiful crystal vanity piece up to the fourth floor. She found a place where she could push it far back into the wall, where nobody living would ever look or find it.

"This is for you," she whispered as a final goodbye. "I hope to encounter you again one day."

Although she felt a strong connection, Casey Caulder never returned to Hill House after it was sold and new people moved in. In closing the tale that she told to this book's author, she pondered the identity of the earthbound spirit she felt such a connection to.

Not knowing the history of the house and its earlier inhabitants, she said, "I feel like her name begins with the letter *L*. It's an old-fashioned name."

Only one woman who lived and died at Hill House fit that description: Louisa Timanus Strawbridge, a well-educated lady who loved the only home she ever owned so much that she remained in it for over 125 years after her death. She perhaps showed herself to some over the years and hid from others, then roamed the ruins until the house was restored and she could once again enjoy it along with the comfort of a living friend who will never forget her.

# 4

# THE MEADE HOUSE

## ELLICOTT CITY

*A spirit of a woman lingers at a stable turned trendy cottage where her son wanted to keep her forever.*

Anyone who has ascended the road past St. Paul's Catholic Church and made a sharp left just past New Cut Road has seen this quaint, brown cottage at 3843 College Avenue. A house with the lowliest of beginnings, the Meade House has been home to a corrections officer, a stenographer, a bakery supply salesman, an eccentric bachelor, a doctor of internal medicine and a university professor. It was also home to the daughter of an Oella millworker who may have remained after her death in the home she lived in and loved for forty-six years.

## THE HISTORY

When the Ellicott brothers moved from Bucks County, Pennsylvania, in 1771, they bought eighty-five acres of land along the Patapsco River, including "The Hollow," where Ellicott City now stands. After the purchase, they divvied up ownership of the property among the brothers and other family members. Among the property was a tract of land on the east side of the Patapsco River called West Illchester that originally belonged to Jonathan Ellicott. The property where the Meade House stands was part of Lot no. 14 on that tract, which may have been carved off in October 1830.

The land seems to have remained in the hands of various members of the Ellicott family until May 15, 1873, when George Ellicott Bros. sold the property to William and Martha Johnson for $1,000. Since the deed didn't mention any improvements on the property, the Johnsons were likely the ones who built a two-story, shingle roofed stable on the site that appears on the 1884, 1887 and 1904 Sanborn Fire Insurance maps.

Since the property was conveniently located across the road from what was then Rock Hill College, the Johnsons' stable may have been where visitors to the academy left their horses. The closest other one was the Dorsey Livery Stable down the hill on Maryland Avenue. The layout of the barn included the current footprint of the Meade House as well as another similar-sized building or wing off the northeastern corner that may have been open-air stalls.

While it's not known whether the Johnsons operated the stable privately or formally leased it to the academy, they officially sold the property and stables to Rock Hill College on June 3, 1890. Presumably, the school continued to use the stables until January 23, 1922, when the college burned to the ground. It was not long afterward that the owners of Rock Hill College had

This simple bungalow was built on an earlier stable's stone foundation. *Howard County Historical Society.*

the property surveyed and divided into six lots in April 1923. They then sold the lots to the Board of Education of Howard County for $13,750 on May 1, 1923, including Lot G, where the Meade House stands.

Maryland tax records show that the Meade House was built in 1920, however, neither a house nor a stable are mentioned in the 1923 deed of sale. It might be that the stables burned down or were demolished—except for one critical part: the foundation.

At least until the 1970s, before it was extensively remodeled, the basement of the Meade House featured a dirt floor, stone stalls and harness hooks of what clearly had been a barn or a stable.

Although the 1923 deed shows that the Board of Education of Howard County had purchased the property, a deed of sale dated June 30, 1925, says that fifty-three-year-old Otto and fifty-five-year old Ida Neumann purchased Lots E, F and G from Rock Hill College with a $3,000 mortgage. This deed mentions improvements, which may mean that the upper-level "house" part had been built before the sale. So, the early 1920s marks the birth of what became the Meade House.

Immigrants from Austria and Germany, the Neumanns moved to the College Avenue home with their twenty-three-year-old daughter Elenore Amelia, who was employed as a stenographer. Although 1920 U.S. Census records show that Otto was working as a trucker, by 1922, he was serving as the warden at the Ellicott City Jail. In the late summer of that year, Neumann and other members of the law-enforcement community apparently helped fend off an attempted jailbreak/lynching of a Black man. The prisoner had been arrested for stealing a watch and subsequently shooting the chief of police in the thigh.

By 1930, Otto and Ida were both dead and Elenore was living alone in the home, which was valued at $7,000. But she didn't live there long. Death came for Elenore at the age of thirty, shortly after her parents had departed this world. Her last will and testament bequeathed the home to William P. Rausch and Company, to sell the house and settle the estate. Rausch almost immediately sold the property to forty-year-old Marion Lee Meade and his wife, Maude May, on August 22, 1931.

Meade and his wife moved into the home at what was then 55 College Avenue along with Maude's mother, Susan Catherine Hobson, seventy; their son Marion, thirteen; and their nephew Robert Irwin Watterfield, six.

The two were longtime locals. Maude May was born in Oella, across the Patapsco from Ellicott City, on May 19, 1894. Her parents were Susan Catherine and John Hobson, a man eleven years her mother's senior.

Twenty-four-year-old Maude May Hobson Meade, circa 1918. *Howard County Historical Society.*

Maude's father and all of her older brothers worked at W.J. Dickey and Sons' Oella cotton and woolen mill, with John Sr. serving as an overseer in the Weaving Room. According to the 1910 U.S. Census, Maude, sixteen, worked the mill as well. She was a spooler, and her twelve-year-old brother toiled as a general runner.

Millwork was hard. John Hobson died in 1919 at the age of seventy after suffering from spinal sclerosis for many years. He is buried in the Oella Cemetery beneath a lovely headstone with an inscription that reads, "His toils are past. His work is done. He fought the fight. The victory won."

In 1913, Maude married Marion Lee Meade, twenty-one. She had known him from childhood. Meade had grown up in Ellicott City, and his father had a barbershop in town. At the time the family moved into the home, he was a bakery-supply salesman for the Ferris-Noeth-Stern Company in Baltimore. Later, he worked as a cashier at Wood & Selick, also in Baltimore.

A newspaper clipping gave an account of the wedding, reporting that Meade, "a diamond hero" on the Oella Baseball Team, and Maude May had visited Baltimore and went to the home of Reverend Kenneth G. Murray of Fayette Street Methodist Episcopal Church to get married. The article ends with a somewhat cryptic observation about Meade: "He has a reputation as a whistler, and has been heard in this city, but baseball, it is said, brought about his downfall as a bachelor."

Three years later, on August 18, 1916, the couple welcomed their only son, Marion Lee Jr., into their lives. Little if anything is known about Marion Jr.'s youth except that he apparently didn't graduate from high school. In 1940, the U.S. Census shows the Meades' twenty-three-year-old son as unemployed and living at his parents' home. Marion enlisted in the military on May 29, 1942. His registration card lists him as being twenty-four years old, unemployed and living on College Avenue, although other military records show his civil occupation as a shipping and receiving clerk. He was inducted into the army as a private. He was five feet, eight inches tall and weighed 112 pounds.

The family lived in the charming, little, three-bedroom, two-bath, shingle-sided cottage for almost fifty years. The nephew, Robert (Jack) Irwin, moved out of the home after graduating from Ellicott City High School around 1942. The grandmother, Susan Catherine, died in 1946, followed by Marion Sr. in 1954—both most likely in the home.

Marion Jr. seems to have remained a lifelong bachelor who continued living at his parents' home after he came home from the service. Described by a neighbor at the time as a "mamma's boy" who may have had some sort of mild mental disability, Marion Jr. took care of Maude May until death carried her away on August 12, 1976. Marion Jr. died of cancer on July 13, 1985.

The house, which had remained the property of Maude's estate, was sold to Alfred Thomas Letle and his wife, Alexandra Joan, on April 29, 1985, for $42,500. It seems the Meade House had been vacant for some time and needed repairs before Alfred and Alexandra could move in with their daughters, Caitlin, seven, and Kristin, three.

Unfortunately, whatever happiness the Letles had at the Meade House was short-lived. A little less than two years after they purchased the home, Alfred signed over his ownership interest in the house to Alexandra on March 28, 1987. The couple divorced in July 1988. Alexandra, who reinstated her maiden name, Paolucci, remained at the home for the next four years until she sold it to Margaret A. Shema on April 9, 1992, for $137,500.

Margaret kept the house until Pablo A. Jimenez and Dr. Sydney E. Jimenez purchased it on April 30, 1996, for $147,500. The house changed hands again in 2002, when Steve Kraemer purchased the property for $215,000. Less than a year later, on January 30, 2003, he sold it to thirty-four-year-old Jeffrey Alan Hedgepeth and his wife, Angela Denise, for $295,000.

The Hedgepeths moved in, but, sadly, the marriage soured. Jeffrey sold his ownership interest in the house to his wife for $49,267.71 on May 18, 2006. Three years later, the house was back on the market. Angela sold the Meade House to Nora and Stephen Park Jr. for $430,000 on November 2, 2009.

The couple lived in the home until 2016, when they sold it to Stephen J. McKenna on December 9 for $420,000. As of this writing, Stephen, a Washington, D.C./Baltimore metro area independent consultant for media analysis, political strategy, speech writing and communications, lives there mostly by himself—except for whatever or whoever it is that keeps him up at night in the little brown house on the corner of College Avenue and Ross Road.

## The Haunting

There are a variety of explanations of why someone's spirit or energy sticks around in a place after their death. Sometimes, it's because the horror of their passing was so intense that it binds them to the place where it happened. Other times, it's a force of habit. They keep doing what they always did in life, over and over again into eternity. Some just can't let go. Their desire to remain in familiar surroundings is stronger than their interest in moving on to the next realm.

The ghost that haunts the Meade House may fall into the last category.

In terms of history, the home has a relatively short one. The list of past owners is brief, with many of the living inhabitants coming and going within a few years. To be sure, some, like Mr. and Mrs. Neumann and their daughter Amelia, most likely passed within the walls of the house, as did the Meades' grandmother Hobson.

Perhaps Marion Meade Sr. did, as well, although by the time he died in 1954, hospital stays at the end of life were more common. However, one life—and one death—stands out for the person's longevity at the home and the disturbing accounts of what may have happened to her after death.

And that's Maude May Hobson Meade.

Legend has it that after Mrs. Meade passed away in the east bedroom of her home sometime in the summer of 1985, Mrs. Ross, a neighbor, came to the door to talk to Marion Jr. Ross hadn't seen Maude May come in or out of the house in weeks, and she was concerned. Marion told her that his mother had been very sick. Her concern heightened, the neighbor asked if she could look in on Maude May. Marion said sure and invited her in.

When Ross entered the home, the smell almost knocked her over.

At the time of Maude May's death, her son Marion was sixty years old. He'd been living there with her alone for thirty years. His mother was likely his sole caretaker and his whole world. When she wouldn't "wake up," it's said Marion didn't know what to do. He may have wanted, more than anything, to have things go back to the way they were.

So, the story goes, when she died, instead of calling the authorities, he closed the door of the east bedroom and left his beloved mother resting on the tidy bed where she had passed into the next world. For how long, nobody knows. It's said that Marion did what he could to keep her decomposing body clean. He sealed and glued newspaper over the windows, floors and walls to hide her from prying eyes and to minimize the odor.

After going upstairs and having her worst fears confirmed, the neighbor called the police to have the body removed. Maude May was buried at St. John's Cemetery next to her husband, Marion Lee Meade Sr.

At least her body went to St. John's. Her spirit seems to have decided that it wanted to stay there at the Meade House.

The Letles, who purchased the home from the Meade estate a few months before Marion Jr. died, were the first to report unsettling happenings at the home. Lights that had been turned on almost immediately were turned off. The TV would turn on and off at odd times, and the family would watch in wide-eyed horror and fascination as an unseen hand slowly rotated the knob, causing the screen to flip through all the channels.

As someone who had once aspired to be a mortician and who had a longtime interest and appreciation for the life after this one, Alexandra Letle wasn't particularly upset by the disturbances, which seemed to occur at least twice a month. Not knowing the name of the departed owner, she and the girls referred to the presence in the home as "Granny."

Granny apparently was possessive of her home and protective of the new living inhabitants. Poltergeist activity would ramp up whenever visitors came. One friend who came to stay over with the girls while Alexandra was away overnight called to say she was packing them up and taking them to her home because of "something" that was in the house. Granny also seemed not to be terribly fond of Alfred, loudly making her presence known when he visited during the couple's breakup.

Maude May's son Marion Meade Jr., sometime between 1940 and 1945. *Howard County Historical Society*.

Although sometimes noisy and disruptive, the ghost of Maude May seemed to be a benevolent spirit—except for one time.

Alexandra was drifting off to sleep in the east bedroom—the room where Maude May died—when she noticed a heavy Chinese checkerboard that was sitting on a chair at the foot of her bed slowly rise into the air.

At the point where it cleared the footboard, Alexandra watched the board fly through the open door and head down the hall to where Caitlin and Kristen were sleeping in their bedroom facing College Avenue.

Suddenly, Alexandra heard a shriek of pain. She ran down the hall to find Caitlin clutching her forehead with blood running down her arm. The board had flown into the bedroom and clipped her across the head so severely that she had to go to the hospital for stitches. As violent as the incident was, it didn't seem to faze the family, who to this day still speak very fondly about the house, "Granny" and the time they spent there.

A subsequent owner, Nora Parks, reported the sound of open-handed slaps on doors, dogs growling at a shadowy figure on the landing and the strange coldness and constantly opening the door of *der schuhgeist* ("a closet in the front"), where she kept her footwear. Others may have their own stories, which, as of this writing remain untold, except for the most recent one.

Here is an account by Stephen McKenna related in an interview with the author:

> *Since I moved to Catonsville, in 1996, and then Ellicott City, I've lived in six houses. Five in Catonsville. All old houses, though my current cabin in Ellicott City is the oldest, one hundred this year. I love this place. Never once in all those old houses did anything strange happen, other than my kids voluntarily straightening their rooms. This house, however, is a live wire. In my four years here, I've had so many weird middle-of-the-night incidents I can't count. Footsteps, closets opening, crazy attic noises, lights going on and off, hanging things falling off the walls. Here's something pretty typical: This past Thursday night I awoke to clattering noises downstairs at 3:14 am (yes, I checked my watch).*
>
> *Then either one or two of the smoke detectors went off. I was like, "Holy shit, there's a fire." Slammed on my [prosthetic] leg and flew downstairs. As soon as I got to the kitchen, the screaming smoke detectors just stopped. And all the lights were on, and cabinets and drawers randomly open. All the doors were bolted. I know I had closed down my kitchen, and I know I had shut off all the lights because I had gone up the stairs to bed around twelve using my phone as a light....I'm one of the most rationalist paranormal skeptics you could ever meet. But I believe there is something going on here.*

That "something" just might be the spirit of Maude May Meade looking after the cottage home her son never wanted her to leave.

# 5

# THE LAWN

## ELKRIDGE

*Ghosts and poltergeists gambol in an eclectic cottage built by an eccentric legal lion.*

Thousands of years before a young attorney built his fanciful summer retreat on Lawyers Hill, Algonquin tribes and enormous herds of elk roamed the hill above the fall line of the Patapsco River that early settlers referred to as the "Ridge of Elk."

Today, this leafy hilltop neighborhood is home to a tight-knit community and a collection of historic nineteenth-century homes that includes The Lawn, a house listed in the National Register of Historic Places at 6036 Old Lawyers Hill Road. Designed by one of the region's true Renaissance men, this local landmark is a home overflowing with fascinating history, fantastical architectural details and playful spirits that do more than go bump in the night.

## THE HISTORY

Sited on a steep hill that rises three hundred feet above the early port town of Elk Ridge Landing on the Patapsco River, The Lawn was built on the first land grant in what is now Howard County.

Known as "Hockley," this one-hundred-acre tract was patented to William Ebden in 1670. After Ebden died in 1677, the property came into the hands of Colonel Edward Dorsey. The tract remained in the Dorsey family until the early 1800s, when members of the Ellicott family purchased the property along with Dorsey iron furnaces.

Toward the middle of the nineteenth century, after the Elk Ridge Landing port had silted in and the iron trade declined, the Ellicotts began selling off property to rich Baltimore families who wanted to build summer homes away from the industrial grime of the city.

The cool, clean, country-like setting wasn't the only thing that made the area so attractive. Thanks to the 1835 construction of the Thomas Viaduct, the oldest multiple-arched, curved railroad bridge in the world, the summer settlement was conveniently connected to the city of Baltimore by rail. Wealthy town-dwellers could leave their homes in the swanky neighborhoods of Bolton Hill and Mount Vernon, board a B&O Railroad passenger car at Mount Clare Station and be sipping iced tea on their veranda after a quick fifteen-minute trip.

Among these upscale urbanites were Baltimore lawyer George Washington Dobbin and his wife, Rebecca Pue, who bought nine acres of "Hockley" from the Ellicotts. A man ahead of his time, Dobbin had been admitted to the bar at the age of twenty-one and was the first attorney to build a home on what would eventually become known as Lawyers Hill.

Reflecting the eclecticism of the era in which it was built and the whims and wide-ranging interests of its owner, The Lawn is a riot of architectural features and styles. It was constructed in three phases over the course of eighteen years.

The first phase, completed in 1842, was a small, rustic, romantic one-and-a-half-story frame cottage featuring a parlor, a dining room, two bedrooms and a spare room on the first floor. The kitchen and servants' quarters were separate from the house.

At the time the home was constructed, the couple had five children: William Bose, who had been born in 1832, Rebecca Pue in 1833, Mary Dorsey in 1836, Robert Archibald in 1839 and George Leonard in 1841. Thomas Murphy would join the family in 1844.

Shortly after his last son was born, doctors advised Dobbin to give up living in the city and permanently move to the quiet of his country home. So, in 1845, he built a large, block-shaped addition along the west wall of the cottage. The new Gothic-inspired space featured fireplaces to warm the house in winter, second-floor rooms, two verandas and a belfry that housed a farm bell. It also included a library with ornate glass-doored bookcases lining all four walls.

The original cottage section of the fantastical home built by G.W Dobbin, circa 1842. *Maryland Historical Trust.*

But he didn't stop there.

Between 1855 and 1865, Dobbin put on another addition to the house, an attached kitchen, as well as incorporated features that reflected his many hobbies and love of gadgetry. At a time when very few people in the world even owned a camera, he not only had one but also built a darkroom and a porch to develop and dry his photographic plates. The space also included a small metalworking shop with an anvil and a rooftop pavilion that functioned as an astronomical observatory. The unusual structure had an eight-foot circular opening in the ceiling to accommodate a telescope, as well as an ingenuous, removable skylight that remains to this day.

The addition also included a huge parlor measuring eighteen by thirty feet anchored by a massive fireplace. Its deep mantle-top shelf was held up by two richly carved supports, each topped by a fox's head.

During that ten-year period of construction, Dobbin's son William Bose, a Baltimore merchant, passed away on March 12, 1864, at the age of thirty-one. Otherwise, the home seemed to be a happy place. As Dobbin's daughter Rebecca Pue Penniman later recounted in the home's listing on the *Maryland Inventory of Historic Places*:

*"We had a very gay house and constant company—plenty of horses and carriages and everything that could add to our pleasure." Choir practice was held every Friday night at The Lawn followed by a generous supper "… which insured the attendance not only of the choir but of some neighbors who came for the social end."*

During the Civil War, the Dobbins were Confederate sympathizers who helped Southerners trying to escape north and shipped medical supplies to help the war efforts in the South. But he also reached his hand across the great divide. In 1869, Dobbin donated land to the community, and residents purchased stocks to build the Elkridge Assembly Rooms, a place where neighbors could set aside their political differences and socialize in a "neutral zone"—a building and a tradition that remains to this day.

By any measure, Dobbin was an extraordinary man.

In 1867, he became a judge on the Supreme Bench of Baltimore. He was dean of the University of Mary School of Law for fourteen years, was a founder of the Maryland Historical Society and served as director of the B&O Railroad. He was also a trustee of the Johns Hopkins University and the Peabody Institute.

The same year Dobbin was seated on the bench, death once again visited The Lawn, suddenly snatching away his youngest son, George Leonard, at the age of twenty-five.

The house returned to its regular rhythms for almost twenty years, until Dobbin's wife, Rebecca, left this temporal life on February 10, 1884. A few years later, after a long and productive life, Judge George Washington Dobbins passed away at The Lawn on May 28, 1891, at the age of eighty-two. He was buried alongside Rebecca at Green Mount Cemetery in Baltimore.

After the judge's death, surviving members of the Dobbin family stayed on. Land was made available to the children and their spouses to build their own cottages on parceled-off pieces of the acreage. The house remained in the family until the judge's unmarried grandson Dr. George Dobbin Brown, an English professor, sold it in 1951.

The new owners, Joe Addison Cobb and Mary "May" Winter Cobb, set about restoring the home, placing it in the National Register of Historic Places in 1984.

During the time the Cobbs owned The Lawn, they rented out portions of the home. Among the tenants were Richard P. and Janice A. Menear, who rented the top floor in the mid-1970s. The couple fell in love with the house.

So, when Joe passed away around 1984, and May Cobb and her son Robert F. Ashleigh put the house up for sale, the Menears pounced on the opportunity. They purchased the quirky, old, historic home on June 27, 1986, for $130,000.

It was a major renovation project. Through research at the Maryland Historical Society, the Menears discovered photos of the interior and decorative exterior finials, which they replicated and installed. Richard rebuilt the bell tower and rang the bell for a neighbor's wedding.

Thirty years after they first began their love affair with the house, the Menears said goodbye to The Lawn, selling it to Christopher Allen and Debra Streeter Allen on April 13, 2006, for $600,000. Later that same year, the house was further rehabbed and featured as Historic Ellicott City Inc.'s 2006 Decorator Show House.

## The Haunting

Whether members of the Dobbin family encountered ghostly presences at The Lawn during the more than one hundred years they lived there isn't known. However, they may have stayed to become one of the spirits and poltergeists that continued to rattle around the home after it passed out of the family's hands.

The Cobbs were the first to report that they felt they weren't alone in their new, old house. Doors and windows would mysteriously lock and unlock themselves. The key to the grandfather clock and sewing scissors would disappear, then show up in their proper places later. Mrs. Cobb also related stories of objects flying off the home's massive mantle, as well as a head of lettuce that levitated off a table in the kitchen where she was preparing dinner. Unfazed, she said the odd occurrences never scared her, because she felt like the spirits that haunted the house were friendly.

The ghosts at The Lawn didn't limit their activities to playing unseen pranks. Late one evening around Easter, a visitor to the Cobbs' home saw two little girls wandering through the halls of the darkened house. At first, he thought it was his daughter and another friend. But when he tried to follow them to send them back to bed, the little girls disappeared. He found his daughter and a friend in a bedroom. Sound asleep.

The spirits made themselves known to the Menears while they were tenants on the third floor. One night, they were awakened by loud scraping sounds coming from behind a newly constructed wall in the kitchen and

Objects have been observed flying off this fabulously carved fireplace mantle. *Maryland Historical Trust.*

other areas of their apartment. When they went to look, no one was there. They returned to bed "shivering for some time under the covers."

In addition to causing trouble with locks on doors and cabinets, the ghosts' mischief also includes breaking a window from the inside and, inexplicably, uprooting flowers from a window box.

So, who are the ghosts that haunt The Lawn?

One clue came from a tenant who used an Ouija board to communicate with the spirits. The board responded that there were several spirits who remained at The Lawn and two other cottages on the property.

Another, more telling clue, came from a six-year-old boy living as a tenant at The Lawn with his parents. When called down to dinner one night, the child responded that he couldn't because he was busy. When they went up to his room, they found him sitting on his bed seeming to be engaged in a conversation with invisible guests.

When they questioned him, the boy responded: "Don't bother me. I'm busy talking to these people."

"What people?" they asked.

The child responded with a list of unfamiliar names that neither the parents nor their son recognized as anyone they knew.

But the spirit people that the boy was talking to knew all of them quite well.

The couple later found out that the names were those of long-dead former residents of The Lawn, Dobbin family members who had passed away but never left and spirits who stayed behind in the unusual house on the hill and seemed eternally happy to share the house they loved with the living.

## 6

# THE SECOND QUAKER SCHOOL HOUSE

## ELLICOTT CITY

*Soon-to-be-resurrected wreck harbors angry haints that hopefully will be laid to rest.*

Visible in many of the earliest photographs of Ellicott City, this often-remodeled stone and shingled-sided building located on Court Avenue next to the towering First Presbyterian Church, now the Museum of Howard County History, may be among the town's oldest structures. Although the circumstances and date of its birth are unclear, the house on Court Avenue was the home where at least three women died and may remain there as mournful, foreboding and even violently angry spirits to this day.

## THE HISTORY

Based on its name, the Second Quaker School House, the natural assumption would be that there was a First Quaker School House. And indeed there was. It was constructed on the east side of the Patapsco River, probably among the little village of homes that surrounded the Ellicott's Mill in the late eighteenth century.

Perhaps because of an increasing number of students, or maybe because the school down near the Patapsco was susceptible to frequent flooding, the Ellicotts built a second schoolhouse on higher ground.

Land records show that the original stone building was erected on a lot atop "Mount Misery" that belonged to Samuel Ellicott, the grandson of Andrew Ellicott, one of the founding fathers of Ellicott City. According to an 1865 account by Martha Ellicott Tyson referencing the two Quaker schools, "the boys were transferred to a stone building next to the Presbyterian Church, facing on Ellicott Street," which is now Court Avenue.

Precisely when it was built is a little murky. A 1905 article by Emily Emerson Lantz referenced the original stone building being "erected by the Ellicott family one hundred years ago." Local lore says that during the early years of the structure's existence it served as a field hospital for soldiers wounded in battles fought in Maryland during the War of 1812, but there seems to be no documented evidence.

In 1910, Brother Fabrician, author of *The History of St. Paul's Church and Parrish*, wrote that the boys were moved to the Second Quaker Schoolhouse in 1820. References that locate the building next to the Presbyterian Church were made long after the church was finished in 1844.

Taking all that into consideration, along with the architectural evidence, it points to a construction date in the very early 1800s. Further proof is that all the historical reports simply say the pupils were transferred to the building, not that it was specifically constructed for that purpose.

During its more than two-hundred-year history, the "old schoolhouse" was substantially transformed by a great number of renovations and remodeling. However, the original building's architectural structure was very simple.

It began as a one-room-deep, three-bay-wide stone structure, meaning it had an entry hall flanked by a room on each side. As can be seen by the stone outline on the west side of the building, it was one or one-and-a-half stories high.

In 1824, "the boys" relocated again, this time to the newly built Rock Hill Academy on College Avenue. Sometime after that, Thomas Hyatt Landsdale and his wife, Harriet Franklin, purchased the property.

Originally from Montgomery County, Thomas had married Harriet on December 10, 1834, in what was then Anne Arundel County. The couple may have purchased and lived in the schoolhouse around that time.

In the years following, they welcomed six children to their family. Samuel Franklin was born in 1835, Richard Hyatt in 1837, Mary Jemima in 1841, Thomas Franklin in 1844, Evan Thomas in 1849 and Elizabeth Franklin in 1850.

According to T.H.S. Boyd in his 1879 book *The History of Montgomery County*, Landsdale started working at the Triadelphia Mills in 1842 until he left to take charge of the Granite Factory at Ellicotts Mills in 1847.

The outline of the original early-1800s, one-and-a-half-story stone structure is visible on the current building. *Howard County Historical Society.*

In 1850, while Landsdale was still running the Granite Factory, he and Harriet sold their home to James M. Miller, fifty-eight, and his wife, Ann, forty-one, for $500.

According to the 1850 U.S. Census, James Miller was employed as a tailor, probably at one of the dress shops in Ellicott City. At some point, James passed on, leaving Ann and their various heirs and executors to sell the home to William Franklin Mayfield, twenty-three, and his wife, Sarah Hudson, twenty, of Baltimore County on March 21, 1866. They welcomed a daughter, Blanche, into their family that same year.

Rare for the time, the Mayfields were a dual-income family with Sarah listed in an 1867 business directory as a hat maker in Ellicott City. Sadly, young Mrs. Mayfield didn't get to enjoy her new home and daughter for very long. She passed away from unknown causes in 1870.

By 1875, William had found love again and married Sarah Hughes of Ellicott City, who may have been employed in a dry-goods store. A year later, in November 1876, they had a daughter they named Maggie.

Tragically, death came knocking at the door of the Second Quaker School House yet again, to claim the life of William's second wife. Whether Sarah died in childbirth or later of some other cause is not known. However grief-stricken he might have been, William continued to long for love and companionship. He found it again with Clentonia "Clennie" H. Atwell, twenty-five, whom he married in 1882.

Within the next few years, Mayfield's daughter Blanche took up a vocation as a nun, eventually ending up as Sister Veronica of the Carmelite Nuns of New Orleans.

William and Clennie remained in the Second Quaker School House for the next fourteen years. During that time, and likely earlier, Mayfield greatly expanded and modified the house.

Sometime in the late nineteenth century, he constructed a two-story frame addition on the north side of the house with a door that opened onto Court Avenue. The simple gable roof on the original building was raised to create a second story with a handsome mansard roof popular at that time. That roof and the three double-hung ornate arched windows can still be seen inside what became a second-story sunroom on the south side of the house.

Then, on January 16, 1896, nearly thirty years after he first moved in, Mayfield decided that their time at the Second Quaker School House was done. On that day, he and Clennie sold the home to Ella Kinsey Getz, thirty-seven, and her German-born husband, Louis N., thirty-seven, for $1,700.

Two interesting side notes before we delve into the Getz ownership. Mayfield's daughter Maggie went on to marry Robert George Yates, the owner of Yates Market. Also, William Mayfield also outlived his third wife, who died in 1907 and was buried alone beneath her own stone at St. John's Cemetery. William Franklin Mayfield lived on until January 13, 1916. He, too, was buried alone at St. John's Cemetery.

The Getzes moved into the Second Quaker School House with their seven-year-old daughter, Mary Elizabeth. According to the 1900 U.S. Census, Louis was a merchant in Ellicott City. In 1910, he was listed as a cashier for a fruit company. In 1920, his occupation was recorded as a bank cashier.

On April 25, 1932, Ella Getz crossed over to the afterlife at the Second Quaker School House. Shortly after, on May 6, Louis drew up a will that would leave the home on its own lot along with two other lots to his daughter Mary Elizabeth, who had married Michael John Weir, and his granddaughter Ella Kinsey Weir.

The Weir family owned the Second Quaker School House until March 28, 1951, when it and three lots were sold by Mary Elizabeth and Michael to the Howard County Board of County Commissioners for $12,500.

Between 1951 and early in 1967, the building was home to the Howard County Planning and Zoning Commission. It then served as the offices of the Howard County States Attorney's Office. At some point, a one-room windowless brick addition was constructed on the east side of the building. Other county offices used it as well.

In September 1986, the Howard County Historical Society took over control of what was known as the Weir Building. The society used it to store its archival collection, including historic photographs and documents, until 2011, when the society moved its archival material and headquarters to the newly built Miller Branch Library.

The society continued to use the now nearly empty Weir Building as storage. For many years, a few of the rooms were rented out to commercial tenants until the society began work on restoring the building to its late nineteenth-century appearance and re-creating its historical "schoolhouse" past as the Children's Museum of Howard County.

# The Haunting

It isn't certain if the spirits that haunt the Second Quaker School House are those of wounded War of 1812 soldiers who may have died within its walls or the departed souls of former owners who took their last mortal breaths there. But the experiences of those who have seen, heard and felt the ghostly presence of those wraiths that remained attached to the building are etched in the minds of those who had them.

The accounts of paranormal activity come from two Museum of Howard County History managers who tell tales of a house supernaturally divided. The right side of the house is peaceful, while the left side both upstairs and down buzzes with a strange energy that causes those sensitive to such things to feel head-pressured, anxious, dizzy and confused.

Few feel comfortable alone in the house. The sensation of being watched is said to be overpowering. One manifestation the managers described as a "black mass" has been seen crossing an upstairs storage room. Another powerful but unseen entity has created a strong enough presence to have blocked people from walking through a doorway into the main second-floor room.

A third experience involved a creeping coldness that came over half of the manager's body and then completely enveloped it with an iciness so intense that his breath crystalized into thick clouds of vapor around his head.

Female voices have often been heard inside the house, including that of a little girl whose materialized specter has been seen standing at the top of the attic stairs.

Most disturbing of all is an intense encounter with an unseen entity during a paranormal investigation in the basement. The manager felt whatever being had been conjured move through him, leaving red marks as if he'd been punched in the face.

Aside from the little girl and the female voices, the presences seem rather ominous. Perhaps they are the Mayfield wives who died at such a young age, angry that their lives were cut short. Maybe the spirits are unhappy that the once lovely home which had been so extensively improved fell into disrepair. If so, it's possible that the ghosts will find peace when the "old schoolhouse" building is brought back to life and is once again filled with the happy voices and laughter of children.

# PART II

# SOUTHERN SPECTERS

# 7

# ATHOL MANOR

## COLUMBIA

*Tragic deaths and desecrated cemeteries wake the dead who won't let the living sleep.*

Here begins Athol, 1730" reads a stone marker at the base of a white oak tree that still stands some distance from what is one of the oldest surviving homes in Howard County. Now clinging to the top of a cutaway hill overlooking six busy lanes of traffic on Route 29 near the Seneca Drive/Shaker Drive interchange, the "English Castle" located at 6680 Martin Road in Columbia is home to nearly three hundred years of history—and a noisy ghost that just wanted to be noticed.

## THE HISTORY

Built between 1730 and 1740, the handsome Georgian-style stone house known as Athol Manor (also Atthole or Athole) was built on the six-hundred-acre land grant of the same name patented to Episcopal minister Reverend James MacGill by King Charles on August 29, 1732.

MacGill (later changed to McGill), who was born in Perth, Scotland, in 1701, had come to America a few years earlier, in 1728, to form a new Church of England in the Maryland colony. He first served as a pastor in Somerset Parish. However, in 1730, he was transferred to Queen Caroline Parish in what was then Anne Arundel County to serve at Christ Church

Guilford. Historically known as the "Old Brick Church," it is the oldest church building still in use in Howard County.

In colonial times, ministers were as much government officials as they were spiritual leaders. So, in addition to leading worship, MacGill would have been responsible for levying poll taxes of tobacco on the taxables of the parish, paying the sheriff's wage and appointing inspectors of tobacco at Elkridge Landing on the Patapsco River. He would have also collected fines from wayward parishioners who failed to show up for mandatory Sunday services.

After "The Parson," as MacGill is referred to in family papers, received his land grant, he quickly set about building his "Mansion House" as the rectory to Christ Church. Constructed of the finest local materials, including granite from a quarry on the property, oak, walnut and pine, the rustic but elegant two-and-a-half-story home reflected the importance of the position the church held within colonial society. It also pays tribute to the craftsmanship of the immigrant Scottish masons and the local enslaved people who built it.

MacGill could certainly afford a fine house. His income from the Church of England–supported parish before the Revolution was about $600 to $1,000 a year, a fortune at that time. The patent he was granted on Athol and other lands he acquired cost him nothing. All he had to pay were one-time fees for the surveys and title papers as well as an annual rent of two shillings (26.66¢ American) for every one hundred acres of land. That would have come to less than $162 a year for the original six-hundred-acre land grant. Undoubtedly, the land was farmed and produced tobacco and other crops that were sold at a profit.

When the house was finished in 1740, Reverend MacGill and his wife, Ellen "Sarah" Hilleary, whom he married in 1730, moved into the home. In accordance with Georgian architectural style, the original part of this lovely house is strictly symmetrical, accented with stone corners, long double-hung windows, central doors on the front and back and stone chimneys at either end. The rooms were spacious. The woodwork was of the finest quality, including the beautiful winding staircase banister where no two spindles were alike. The basement kitchen boasted a cavernous fireplace and three beehive ovens topped by a one-and-a-half-foot slab of solid granite.

Then, 232 years after Athol was completed, a historical researcher named James C. Wilfong spotted the initials "JMS" and the date "1740" cut deeply into one of the granite windowsills. The letters signified "James MACGILL Sarah."

Reverend MacGill's "English Castle" was built by Scottish stonemasons and enslaved laborers. *Maryland Historical Trust.*

The MacGills brought their growing gaggle of children with them to the home: James (nine), Thomas (seven), John (five), Sarah (three) and Eleanor (one). A year later, daughter Margaret Ann arrived, and after that, in 1744, came another son, Patrick. Sadly, the little boy didn't live long, dying just five days after his first birthday. In 1746, daughter Anne was born, but the joy of her birth was also short-lived. Anne followed her brother to the family graveyard before she turned one. After that, the MacGills had two more daughters: Mary, born in 1749, and Caroline, born in 1753. Unfortunately, death wasn't quite done with the MacGill children. In 1758, Eleanor was tragically taken at the age of nineteen. Her cause of death is unknown.

The reverend and Sarah then settled into the last part of their lives. "The industrious parish minister," as described by the Reverend Alexander Adams in a letter to the Bishop of London dated September 29, 1752, continued to serve as pastor at Old Brick until he had to retire in 1776. At that time, the English government cut off support to the churches in the colonies because of the American Revolution. On October 20, 1779, he passed away, likely with his wife of nearly fifty years at his side. Sarah would live on until 1791, when she joined the parson and three of their children in the family graveyard on the property.

By the time he died, MacGill had accumulated a vast amount of land. The final tally was 837 acres, including land grants known as "New Year's Gift," "Brown's Hopyard," "William's Lot" and "Scanthings Lot" that were combined and renamed "Athole Enlarged" in 1763. It's said that after MacGill's death, the ownership of the Athol plantation house and its hundreds of acres of land was bitterly contested among his heirs, who parceled it off to various buyers.

Convoluted land records that span the next one hundred years show a procession of owners with names that include Shipley, Moxley, Worthington (of John), Hammond, Phelps, Gorman, Clarke, Holland, Dixon and others who picked off little bits and big pieces of Athol's rapidly dwindling carcass.

In 1897, the property was sold at a public auction for $3,200 to Jennie M. Geaslen. On January 11, 1902, Jennie and her husband, James Stocker, sold Athol and 162 acres to Clarksville-area farmer John William Stromberg and his wife, Annie, for $4,300. In 1920, the Strombergs purchased an additional 20 acres of the original land grant to enlarge the property to nearly 200 acres.

In 1927, their son Paul Edward Stromberg, who, contrary to other reports, wasn't the owner and publisher of the *Howard County Times*, sold the property to Melvin and Mildred Coar. By then, the Great Depression was looming on the horizon. Over the next thirty years, Athol was bought and sold numerous times, with the acreage decreasing with almost every sale. The formerly grand estate and its grounds fell into a sad state of disrepair. It was a tragedy for both the home and the departed souls of Athol.

In addition to being an important historical property, Athol was also the final resting place of Reverend MacGill and likely most of his family. Originally, the property was the site of two private cemeteries. One was located to the north of the house. The other was located to the east. In 1942, when the property was owned by the Coars, the little family cemetery at Athol was being used as a hog lot. At the time, only three tombstones were left standing. One was broken almost in half. All of the stones were rounded at the corners from the hogs using them as scratching posts. Reportedly, none bore the MacGill name.

At that time, some MacGill family descendants discussed trying to move whatever family remains could be found to the graveyard at Christ Church. After cemetery experts told them they doubted much would be left to reinter, they abandoned the project.

The Coars sold the property to Walter van Durand in 1946. When the land that contained the north cemetery was sold to Louis and Grace Brown in the early 1950s, what was left of the bodies in that graveyard were dug up and reinterred elsewhere. It's said that when the graves were opened for the bodies to be moved, someone out of curiosity opened one of the smaller caskets that may have been the final resting place of either MacGill's young son or daughter who died in the 1740s.

When the coffin was pried open, the bystanders looked down into it in stunned silence. The casket was empty. There was no skeleton. No scraps of clothing. No jewelry. Nothing physical remained. Nothing, except the faint outline of the body of a small child on the fabric lining of the coffin. After that, any curiosity the bystanders had about the contents of the caskets was killed and no others were opened.

About that time in 1952, Thomas H. Dike and Edwina S. Dike bought Athol from the Browns and another portion from Walter and Ann C. Van Durand. The formerly abandoned house that had been used to store hay now stood on just seven remaining acres of the original six-hundred-acre land grant. It began to be reborn under the stewardship of the Dikes. In addition to working to restore the home to its original mid-eighteenth-century appearance, they constructed a significant random stone addition to the house.

In the 1970s, after part of the subdivided estate was purchased by the Rouse Company, two of the tombstones in the other burial ground that were still standing were moved for residential development on the eastern side of Route 29. However, this time, none of the bodies were moved. All of the bodies in the marked and unmarked graves in the eastern graveyard stayed where they had been originally buried. The location of what was left of the mortal remains of the early MacGill family is unknown. They may well lie beneath the pavement of Route 29 or under the basements of the homes in the Macgill's Common, Huntington and Dickinson neighborhoods. There are some accounts of an overgrown, abandoned cemetery located at the edge of the Kings Contrivance property.

The Dikes maintained Athol until 1986, when they sold the house to W. Clark and Carolyn L. Gaughan. In 1997, a historical survey recommended the property be added to the National Register of Historic Places because of its significant contributions to history, architecture and artistic merit. Although the recommendation was denied, Athol continued to be well-loved.

In 1999, Lisa M. Smith bought the home for $350,000. Michelle Lynn Armstrong next purchased the property for $525,000 in 2011. Five years later, Armstrong sold Athol on its .9200-acre sliver of land to Legacy Investments LLC on October 6, 2016, for $625,000. Future plans for the property are unknown at this time.

# THE HAUNTING

A nearly three-hundred-year-old house with two family graveyards on the property that have been disturbed and desecrated almost can't help but be haunted. And Athol does not disappoint.

Deep in the dark middle of the midnight hour, unexplained noises have been heard on what was reported to be almost a nightly basis. Described as a rhythmic "click, click, click" by the unsettled homeowners, it sounded like someone running a stick or a ruler along the spiraling spindles of the beautiful stairway banister, much like a child running a stick along a picket fence.

Sounds from this spooky spindle staircase woke the living from a dead sleep. *Erica Zoren.*

Who might it be?

Little Patrick and Anne MacGill, who died in the 1740s, each left this life when they were about one year old—far too young to be a ghost toddling downstairs with a stick in their hand. Perhaps it was Eleanor, the MacGill daughter who died at the age of nineteen, ascending the stairs of her parents' beautiful home simply trying to make her presence known.

Curious clicking sounds weren't the only manifestations disturbing the sleep of those living upstairs at Athol. A rocking chair in the master bedroom would creak into motion, slowly and steadily moving back and forth, night after night. Was it Mrs. MacGill trying to soothe the grief of losing two young children, a daughter and, finally, her husband in the waning years of her life?

No one can be certain, but the "unseemly incidents" unnerved the owners so much that, as Catholics, they called in a local priest for help in quieting whatever "presence" was haunting the halls of Athol. In an effort to comfort them, it's said that the priest "exorcised" the home. After that, the clicking stopped and the chair finally remained as still as the grave the ghost may have risen from.

Considering the graveyards on the property that are full of souls who lived and died at Athol over nearly three centuries, the spirit could have been anyone from a family member to one of the dozens if not hundreds of enslaved people who worked on the plantation. One thing is certain: Although the inhabitants of Athol have disappeared into the mists of eternity, the sturdy stone house they called home still stands, awaiting a major renovation—and another chapter in its long history.

# 8

# THE KINGS CONTRIVANCE

## COLUMBIA

*Sited on a royal land grant, a notorious restaurant remained a home*
*a country girl could never leave.*

Once accessed directly from Route 32 when it was a two-lane country road, the 1900-era house known as the Kings Contrivance is located at 10150 Shaker Drive. The gracious granite structure has deep roots in Howard County history, a ghastly legend and ghostly presences that terrorized the staff of the home-turned-restaurant for three decades.

## THE HISTORY

The history of the house that would become known as the Kings Contrivance is intimately intertwined with that of Athol and the six-hundred-acre land grant of the same name that was patented to Reverend James MacGill by King Charles on August 29, 1732.

In 1780, Reverend MacGill constructed a stone building facing east on the site of the modern-day Kings Contrivance home. Nearly one hundred years later, in 1870, the size of the stone building was doubled to create a much larger frame house that was topped by a mansard roof and embellished with Victorian elements.

Unfortunately, in 1899, that house burned to the ground and the remains of the house were demolished. Residents who moved into the MacGill's Common, Huntington and Dickinson neighborhoods when the land was developed in the 1970s reported finding old doorknobs, hinges and other debris in fill dirt that may have been part of the old house.

In 1900, the stately Federal-style house that stands today was built on the site, presumably by someone in the MacGill family, possibly Richard Gambrill MacGill Jr.

The front of the now western-facing home features a one-story-high, flat-roofed portico supported by four wood Doric columns and a balustrade. The interior of this impressive turn-of-the-century home features a central hall and an open staircase with turned spindles that originally ascended from the ground floor to the attic. Two large rooms flank the center hall, which has a fireplace on the north wall.

Before the advent of central heat, the house had to be toasty in the winter, because the north parlor, which was originally the Billiard Room, accommodates the warming blazes of two additional corner fireplaces. The mantle on the northeast corner of the room is ornamented with fluted pilasters with ovals, urns and garlands, while the mantle in the northwest corner simply features fluted half-columns.

The southwest room has yet another large fireplace on its east wall with paneling to the ceiling over the mantle. The southeast room is graced with an additional large fireplace with a mantle flanked by half-columns. Most all of the rooms on the first floor are decked out with impressive wood moldings, chair rails, door frames and lintels.

Some records show that the presumed builder of the Kings Contrivance house, Richard Gambrill MacGill Jr., married Anne Stuart MacGill—possibly a relative—in Virginia in 1903. She died shortly thereafter at Athol in 1904. Specific details on her death are shrouded in mystery.

Clearer records indicate that five years later, in 1909, Richard Gambrill MacGill Jr., forty-three, married Rachel Cook Clarke, twenty-eight, of Howard County. Legend has it that one day when Richard was working on the estate, he injured himself fairly significantly on some barbed wire and that their love affair blossomed during the time she nursed him back to health.

The U.S. Census shows Richard living in Baltimore before this time, so the beautiful house may have been his country home. In 1910, the records show the couple lived on Columbia Road, possibly at Athol, along with his seventy-year-old mother and forty-year-old sister Annette, perhaps while the home was being renovated for the newlyweds.

A few years later, their son Richard was born in 1911. James came along in 1913, and daughter Elizabeth arrived in 1915. Although the census shows the family living in Baltimore in 1920, accounts of James's life say that he spent his boyhood years at their Howard County country home. Sadly, just fourteen years after the birth of his daughter, Richard passed away on May 22, 1929. Some records say he died in an upstairs bedroom at the manor home, although newspaper accounts list Baltimore as his place of death.

James, the most accomplished of Richard and Rachel's children, graduated from Johns Hopkins University and went on to earn his law degree from the University of Baltimore before starting a general law practice in Ellicott City. In 1946, he married Mary Herbert Buckler, and the couple, along with Sally Keene Craig, Mary's daughter from a previous marriage, moved into what was called "the manager's house" on the grounds of his childhood home. However, they only stayed a short time before moving away. In 1954, Governor Theodore McKeldin appointed MacGill to the position of circuit court judge. He retired in 1980.

While her children went off to pursue their professional lives, Rachel remained at her beautiful home managing the family's dairy farm for the rest of her life. It's said she passed away in her sleep there on December 2, 1959, at the age of seventy-eight. Some reports say that because the staff had been dismissed or had quit, her body wasn't discovered until sometime later. It's said the mailman alerted the police after mail started piling up at the door.

After her death, the 370-acre farm passed into the hands of her children, who sold the property to American diplomat, businessman and philanthropist Kingdon Gould Jr. A graduate of Yale University who had gone to Washington, D.C., to practice law and become a prominent member of the Republican Party, Gould longed to live in the country. A newspaper account said he used a compass to draw a circle thirty miles around the White House to decide where to live. At the northern end of his range, he found Overlook, which had been the home of U.S. senator Arthur P. Gorman. Eight years after purchasing the estate in 1952, Gould bought the MacGill home and property to turn into a restaurant and hunt club, which opened in 1962.

In the course of buying his properties, Gould reviewed old Howard County land grants, including one called "Warfield's Contrivance." He liked the word *contrivance* (which means the use of skill to bring something about or create something) so much that he decided to combine it with his nickname, "King," and christened his restaurant the Kings Contrivance.

Once a gracious country home, the Kings Contrivance is currently an upscale restaurant. *Maryland Historical Trust.*

Thanks to its location near yet just far enough away from Washington, D.C., as well as Gould's ties to bigwigs in the Republican Party, the elegant country retreat became a popular destination for wealthy jet-setters, local luminaries and international dignitaries. In fact, the secluded getaway was reported to be a favorite spot for D.C. politicians who wanted to spend a romantic evening alone with their illicit mistresses.

Night after night in the gracious halls of the old MacGill home, waiters in powdered wigs served exotic wild game and other colonial-themed dishes to guests, reportedly including Richard Nixon and John F. Kennedy.

After seven years of presiding over the mystery, romance and intrigue of his storied restaurant, Gould sold the property to the Howard Research and Development Company/The Rouse Company, which was then in the process of creating the utopian town of Columbia.

The interesting thing is that he didn't actually sell it directly to Rouse.

On December 13, 1966, the Kings Contrivance property as well as dozens of other properties totaling 13,690.611 acres were sold to a woman named

C. Aileen Ames. A trusted longtime Rouse Company secretary, she served as a "straw buyer" for properties that the company was purchasing to form Columbia. On that day, C. Aileen Ames for "a split-second in time" owned every square foot of land in Howard County that Rouse had assembled since October 30, 1963—$18 million worth.

In the 1970s, Howard Research and Development and the Columbia Association had plans to build a thirty-five-acre, eighteen-hole golf course as part of the future development of the Kings Contrivance village. But, due in part to the recession of 1973–75, it was never built. At some point, the property was acquired by Columbia Mall Inc., which sold it to Kings Court LLC in 2002 for $1.2 million. As of this writing, the Kings Contrivance restaurant continues to serve guests as a favorite destination for special-occasion dining—as well as the place where the last sightings of its former owners are remembered

# The Haunting

From the time the Kings Contrivance restaurant opened in 1962, just a few short years after the death of Mrs. MacGill, both staff and guests began hearing unexplained noises and seeing things other than the dessert cart rolling down the halls of the mansion.

Perhaps the least ominous manifestation is the whistling. Heard by staff members as well as a startled painter, the cheery notes have been heard to ring out when no one but the listener is in the building. Since Mrs. MacGill grew up in an era when the adage "a whistling woman and a crowing hen always come to some bad end" was popular, most attribute the musical sounds to her husband checking in on things at his old home.

A dishwasher who worked there in the 1970s said he always felt uncomfortable there closing on Saturday nights. He said that he often found the basement door ajar after he knew he had closed it. Others have seen the wispy form of a woman there who disappeared into walls of the stone foundation.

Culinary staff reported strange goings-on in the kitchen. Pots and pans would be found mysteriously moved from where they had been put away. Coffee pots that had been turned off at night would be found merrily perking away in the mornings when the restaurant opened up. The oven also had a habit of heating up on its own.

Most attribute the sounds and poltergeist activity to the departed residents of the house, but others point out the cemetery that is said to be located under a tangle of honeysuckle and weeds way out to the back left of the five-acre property. Some remember remnants of tombstones—one with the name Jesse Hanes on it—but now many say nothing remains but indentations where the graves are. Riders ambling past the cemetery on horseback say their horses would spook, pick up the pace and become restless when they passed by. One said she remembered a cradle hanging in the boughs of a big tree.

Most common is a general heavy, overbearing feeling. Some swear that they've heard that Mrs. MacGill's body was actually found during the initial renovation, boarded up in one of the walls. It is her apparition that most people say they've seen.

Longtime maître d' Richard Ackman had numerous experiences over the years. Once, he saw a figure glide down the stairs from the second floor and disappear into one of the rooms. He followed it, sensing an unseen presence walking ahead of him as he went from room to room.

Another time, another maître d' and one of the chefs heard unexplained noises upstairs. When they went to investigate, they heard the name "Paul" (which was both their names) being screamed and saw a ball of light rolling down the hall. Ackman, too, experienced lights crackling in the carpet in Richard MacGill's bedroom.

The home-turned-restaurant has a small apartment on the third floor where a chef lived for a while. One night after the restaurant had closed and all the staff had gone home, he had an uneasy feeling. Worried that he might have forgotten to lock a door or turn something off, he crept down the stairs to check things out. When he descended to the first floor, he saw flickering lights that drew him to the veranda dining rooms. There he found every candle on all of the tables lit and blazing away. He stood there shocked, since he knew they had been extinguished hours before. After hurriedly blowing the candles out, he quickly ran up the stairs and locked the apartment door behind him. In the morning when he came downstairs, he cautiously went to look in on the veranda. He was relieved to see that all of the candles were still out—but then he stopped in his tracks. On closer inspection, his blood ran cold.

All the candle wicks that had been lit when he came down in the middle of the night were pristine and mysteriously unburned.

On other occasions, the ghostly presence was not so subtle.

One night in 1972, when an employee was closing up and the last one out of the building, he says he was about fifty feet out the door when he had an uncomfortable feeling. He turned around and was shocked to see an elderly woman staring down at him from an upstairs window. He knew he was alone, because the night watchman who lived above the kitchen was at his girlfriend's house that night. The next day, he told the manager about the experience.

The manager paused and confided that one snowy night when he had stayed at the apartment because the roads were too bad to get home to Baltimore, something happened.

Just as he was about to drift off to sleep in the snowy silence of the great house, he looked up to see the specter of a woman. She had white hair and was wearing a white gown as she slowly walked through the locked apartment door. He lay there paralyzed with fear as she approached the bed. She stopped and stood there staring down at him. He said he pulled the sheets up over his head and waited a few minutes. When he got the courage to peek out from under the covers, she was gone.

The appearances, noises and mysteriously moving objects continued unabated until 1989. Thirty years after Mrs. MacGill departed this life at the Kings Contrivance, the owners did a major renovation on her old home. The wallpaper was ripped down. Carpeting was pulled up and replaced. All the bathrooms were redone.

And whether it was because she no longer recognized the home where she had spent seventy-eight years of life and thirty more after death, or because she saw the light that would lead her to peace, the last wisps of Rachel Cook Clarke MacGill disappeared into the mists of eternity. All the manifestations at the Kings Contrivance ceased, and the house returned to the serenity Mrs. MacGill must have loved when she was alive.

# 9

# Savage Mill

## Savage

*Cheerful spirits defy a former factory's history of death,
dismemberment and bitter disappointments.*

Now an entertainment venue where children happily lick ice-cream cones and shriek with delight as they glide down zip lines, the two-hundred-year-old Savage Mill, located at 8600 Foundry Street, has a dark history born of its industrial past. Inside its looming tower, cavernous former workrooms and warren of artist studios, the spirits of child laborers and employees who perished in the ghastly gnashing machinery live on after death. Ghostly laughter, the sound of skipping steps and the occasional push of a prankster continue to haunt a reborn factory where cotton was loomed, fortunes were made and lost and Santa came to town.

## The History

The property that Savage Mill stands on was originally part of a land grant called "Ridgeley's Forest," which was surveyed on June 3, 1685, by Colonel Henry Ridgely. In its earliest days, Alexander Warfield's son lived on the property but then transferred it to his cousin Alexander Warfield (of John) who built the first mill on the falls of the Patuxent. His sons Brice Warfield and John Worthington inherited the mill, but it ran into financial trouble. They sold it to Francis Simpson along with parts of what was called "Warfield's Range" in 1760.

Despite the failure of the earlier mill, the site on the rapids of the Little Patuxent River was a good one. In the early 1800s, John Savage bought five hundred acres of the property, which was located near what was called "White's Contrivance." In 1821, he, along with John Adams Williams and his brothers George, Amos and Cumberland, as well as other associates, chartered the Savage Manufacturing Company to make and sell cotton goods. In addition to providing the land, Savage loaned money to start the enterprise and held a mortgage on the property.

The Williams brothers and Savage took the mill operation bigtime. They built an entire factory complex in the Federal style, including the main cotton mill, flour mills and sawmills, and a warehouse. The oldest structure is the stone carding and spinning building. Since it was estimated to have been built between 1816 and 1823, the original three-story building may have been on the property when it was purchased. Later, a brick fourth story was added, along with an open belfry featuring a domed roof.

By 1825, the mill had two hundred men, women and children operating 120 power mills. During that era, they expanded the complex to include the addition of a gristmill, a machine shop and an iron foundry.

Unfortunately, because Savage Mill was highly leveraged by debt, the success of the enterprise was on shaky financial ground from the start. After John Savage died in 1847, his heirs ended up selling the entire thing lock, stock and barrel to William H. Baldwin Jr.

Baldwin was a good man for the job. He owned Woodward, Baldwin and Company, a successful dry-goods marketing company in Baltimore. Under his steady hand, Savage Mill regained its footing. The iron foundry, which had been shut down, fired up its forges once again and focused on the production of cotton mill machinery.

In 1914, the operation became Baldwin, Leslie and Company. It added a 123,000-square-foot weaving room to produce cotton duck for use in World War I. By the 1930s, the complex had expanded significantly and featured sixteen factory buildings, including a picking and spinning building, a wheelhouse, a boiler house, an officer's house, as well as branding, storage and shipping buildings.

By 1941, Savage Mill employed 325 people. At the height of World War II production, it turned out 400,000 pounds of cotton duck a month. When the war ended, so did the mill's prosperity. In 1947, the mill and the entire town were sold to Harry Harrison Heim for $450,000. The new

The historic cotton mill's most notorious ghost may not be who most people think she is. *Steve Freeman*.

owner moved his Santa Novelties company to the mill, which, while it was in operation, produced as much as one-third of all the handblown ornaments sold in the United States.

Heim threw himself into his Christmas ornament business and even went so far as to try to change the name of the town to Santa Heim, Merriland. (The legislature declined to make it official.) Nevertheless, he made a proclamation that the town would be Santa's home (*heim* is German for "home") south of the Mason-Dixon line and operated it as a year-round Christmas village.

On December 11, 1948, he launched his fabulous enterprise with a "one-ring" circus in the mill's New Weave Room. Apparently, it was quite the spectacle. There were elephants, trapeze artists and a merry-go-round. Local children dressed as Mother Goose story characters, and over twenty-eight thousand multicolored lights strung throughout the town added to the festive air. He even brought in live reindeer to graze on the lawn behind the Baldwin Hall community center, which he had turned into a toy store.

At the grand opening, Maryland governor Preston Lane gave a speech to a crowd of over ten thousand people, including children brought in from Baltimore and Washington, D.C., on three special B&O Railroad trains dubbed the "Santa Heim Special."

Things got a whole lot less merry after that first Christmas.

In April 1949, Harry Heim was indicted for tax evasion. Fortunately, he got off with paying the back taxes and a $100 fine. His luck was short-lived. When thousands of excited visitors showed up at Santa Heim for its December 4 Sunday opening for the Christmas season later that year, they were disappointed to find the wonderland closed by the authorities. It seems Santa's southern home was found to violate the county's 1723 blue law, which prohibited operation on Sundays.

Santa himself must have intervened. Just four days later, on December 8, 1949, Daniel M. Murry Jr., the state attorney for Howard County, ruled that Santa Heim could open its doors on Sundays, with one catch. All of its proceeds from Sunday sales had to be donated to charity.

Not a recipe for financial success.

Hobbled, the enterprise stumbled on, only to be dealt yet another blow exactly one year later, on December 8, 1950.

On that date, the fire marshal shut down Santa Heim's Christmas Carnival. It seems that 70 percent of one of the tents was made of highly flammable material, and the electrical wiring was dodgy. After removing the wiring and covering the walls with a fireproof lining, the tent was back in business two days later.

That was pretty much it for Santa Heim. After the end of its third season, it closed forever. Heim was deeply in debt, and after World War II ended, overseas manufacturers started making cheaper ornaments.

Santa Heim and Santa Novelties Inc. shut down for good on March 27, 1951. Everything went up for sale. The factory, the ornament-making machinery and the entire town were sold off. Heartbroken, Harry Heim held on to life for only a few more years. The impresario of Santa Heim died on February 1, 1953, at the age of sixty-nine, leaving behind shards of broken dreams and handblown Christmas ornaments.

After Heim's glorious experiment faded into darkness, Albert Winer and his brothers Samuel, Hyman and Ephraim bought the property and used it as a warehouse for the National Store Fixture Company for almost three decades. Toward the end of that period, the Winers began restoring the mill. In 1985, Albert Winer's son Jay founded Savage Limited Partnership. He reopened the mill as a collection of restaurants, specialty shops, artists' studios and antiques dealers. In its heyday around 2010, the reincarnated Savage Mill was drawing one million visitors a year. In following years, the popularity of the mill seemed to decline, perhaps due in part to the decreased interest in antiques, which at one point made up the bulk of the venue's offerings.

But while interest in old stuff may have fallen off, the public's fascination with the dead and only partially departed spirits of Savage Mill remains high. Regular ghost tours continue to draw both the skeptical and superstitious to venture into the dark halls and former factory floors of this two-hundred-year-old industrial complex.

# THE HAUNTING

From the eerie ringing of a phantom bell in the now-empty tower and odd occurrences in the paymaster's office, to the disembodied voices of the dead calling out the names of the living, Savage Mill seems to be packed with paranormal activity.

Only a few of the ghosts of Savage Mill are adults. One is the specter of a man seen hanging from a noose in a loft window of one of the buildings. Another is said to be the wandering ghost of Rebecca King, who died when she slipped on a spool and broke her neck falling down the steep steps of the mill's iconic tower. Most of the spirits appear to be children.

Whether it's laughter, crying or the plaintive cry of a spirit that has been heard pleading "Ma, come home!" the mill is teeming with the spiritual remains of those who were torn away from this world much too soon.

And it's little wonder.

At the end of the eighteenth century, a little more than twenty years before the looms of Savage Mill began turning out cotton canvas, a national newsweekly magazine, the *Niles Register*, said that factory work wasn't for adult men, but instead was "better done by little girls from six to twelve years old." This is why the mill owners made machines so easy to use that a child could operate them. They actually thought factory work was good for children and society.

In fact, an 1802 ad in the Baltimore *Federal Gazette* was looking for children aged twelve to eighteen to work in a local cotton mill. The ad read, "It is hoped that those citizens having a knowledge of families, having children destitute of employment, will do an act of public benefit by directing them to the institution [cotton mill]."

The littlest children might start out as scavengers, crawling underneath the machinery to clear away debris and collect cotton that might have dropped to the floor. As you might imagine, such work was incredibly dangerous. The moving parts of the machines often ripped out their hair, broke their arms and fingers, cut off their heads or crushed their tiny bodies.

Losing children on the factory floor was just the cost of being poor in the American industrial age. Fortunately, child-labor laws were eventually enacted, and the horrors of earlier days were lessened over the course of the mill's 120-plus-year operating life.

Among the site's most famous and mischievous ghosts is said to be Frances Reeley. Legend has it that she was the young daughter of William Bryan Reeley, who served as vice-president and the last manager of Savage Mill in the 1940s. She's been heard laughing and merrily skipping along the old wood floorboards in various parts of the mill.

Little Frances is known as a prankster. A playful spirit, she is fond of tripping visitors on the third step from the bottom of the stairway that leads up and out of the mill's main hall. Although the haunted tread has been repeatedly examined for irregularities by the owner's insurance company because of the frequency of the mishaps, nothing has ever been found amiss. Yet visitors and employees alike continue to mysteriously catch the toe of their shoe on the step and pitch headlong onto the stairs in front of them—much to the delight of the invisible little "tripster."

So why would the ghost of the young daughter of the wealthy mill manager haunt her father's workplace? Surely, she didn't die there toiling as a child laborer in the 1940s. And, indeed, there is no record of Willian Bryan Reeley and his wife, Esther Ritchie McElvaney, ever having a daughter named Frances. The daughters they did have were named Elizabeth, Beulah and the youngest, Esther Irma, who died in 2009.

So as romantic as the story is and as real as Frances might have been in life—and now in death—we don't know for sure who the child actually was. Interestingly enough, historical records do provide some tantalizing clues. It seems there was a little girl, Frances S. Reeley, who was born in 1930 in Guilford, Maryland, very near Savage Mill. Her parents were Grace and Jenning Bryant Reeley. Jenning may have worked with his brother William at an auto factory. At the time, baby Frances and her family were living with her grandfather Richard Reeley, seventy-two, who even at that age was still working as a mail carrier.

All we know for sure is that this Frances S. Reeley, who the U.S. Census says was born in 1930, never appears in the records again.

Additionally, when her father Jenning died in 1957, his obituary listed only Frances's sister Jean as a surviving child. Perhaps it was this little girl who worked there, or maybe visited the mill with her father or grandfather. Maybe she somehow got away from them to run happily across the factory floor and slipped and fell into the machinery. Maybe it was she who tragically died as a young child and, despite the pain and sorrow, remains behind at Savage Mill as a happy spirit to this day.

# PART III

# WESTERN WRAITHS

# 10

# The Gerwig-Lintner House

*The spirit of a murdered woman disturbs a daycare center
on the site of an old farmhouse.*

Once located on the southwest corner of Route 144 and Centennial Lane, the Gerwig-Lintner House stood on the site now occupied by La Petite Academy at 10101 Frederick Road. Today, the lovely home, which had weathered the ravages of time, the sadness of a five-generation family who had to leave it and the gut-wrenching death of the woman who worked so hard to bring the house back to life, is now gone from the physical world. However, it has not been forgotten by many of the living and, apparently, at least one of the dead.

## The History

Constructed around 1830, the rustic stone-and-frame Gerwig-Lintner House was built by German immigrant Jacob Frederick Gerwig Sr. Born in 1793, Gerwig and his wife, Christina Catharina Lehmann, who was born in 1801, grew up in Wurtemburg, Germany. On December 19, 1829, the young couple and their four children—Matthaus (six), Jacob Frederick Jr. (five), Christina (three) and Frederick (one)—boarded a boat in Neuenburg, Germany, and set out to find their fortune in America. They arrived by ship at the port of Baltimore in early 1830.

Industrious by nature, the Gerwigs wasted little time in settling into their new home. A few months after they arrived in America, they headed southwest of Baltimore to what was then Anne Arundel County. There, they purchased one hundred acres of land that was part of the original seven thousand acres patented to Charles Carroll I ("The Settler") in 1702 as "Doughoreagan." Later, in 1717, the patent was expanded to ten thousand acres and renamed "Doughoreagan Manor."

Located in an area known as Pine Orchard, just 3.6 miles west of Ellicott City, the Gerwig farm bordered on Centennial Lane at the east and extended about three-quarters of a mile, where it met the eastern edge of the Carroll estate. There, Jacob, whose occupation is listed as a carpet weaver in U.S. Census records, built a simple four-bay-wide, one-room deep, two-and-a-half-story, German-siding frame house with a center chimney.

With a new child arriving almost every year, the Gerwig family was growing fast. They later added a one-room deep, two-story-high fieldstone structure to the frame house. Their son John, the first child to be born in America, came along in November 1830, followed by Godfried in 1832, Charles in 1834, William in 1835 and Caroline in 1838. Emily came along in 1840 and George in 1842. Finally, Louis rounded out the family, arriving on the Gerwig farm on January 16, 1845. Fortunate for the times, they only lost two children. Nine of the boys and one of the girls survived into adulthood.

Over the years, the Gerwig family added a front porch and a rear porch that was eventually replaced by a large kitchen. Sometime during the late nineteenth century, a small apartment was built onto the eastern side of the home. During the Civil War, their oldest son, Matthaus, served as a corporal in the Third Regiment, West Virginia Cavalry. He came back home in June 1865, in time to be there on December 21 when his mother, Christina, passed away at the Pine Orchard farm.

By then, their son Frederick Jacob Jr. was head of the household, fathering six children with his wife, Mary Louise. In 1871, Frederick had a gable roof and Roman-arched dormer windows added to the top of the house, possibly constructed by a craftsman by the name of J. Yingst, who inscribed his name and the date on his finished handiwork.

In 1885, the family patriarch, Jacob Frederick Sr., followed his wife to the grave at the ripe old age of ninety-two. He had outlived his son Jacob Frederick Jr., who died on November 29, 1884, by one year. Father and son, as well as many other family members, were buried at Louden Park

A heinous crime stains the site where this 1800s farmhouse once stood. *Maryland Historical Trust.*

Cemetery in Baltimore beneath rather fancy headstones. At that point, Jacob Jr.'s son John Henry and his wife, Florence Ardella Grimes, then headed up the fourth generation of Gerwigs at the farm on Route 144.

John Henry and Ardella had five children: Harry Thomas, John Monroe, Charles Joseph, William Jacob and Bradley Monroe. William Jacob, born on September 1, 1909, married Miriam Brown. He would be head of the household of the fifth and final generation to live at the Gerwig farm. William Jacob came into the property in 1937 after his parents' deaths, when the family decided to sell outright the farm, house, outbuildings and livestock to him at a low price. Their children William and, later, Ardella, would be the last children to be born at the old house while they struggled to make a go of the farm.

In the end, it was just too hard. The nation was still struggling to get out of the Depression and was in the middle of World War II. Laborers left the farm for high wages, short hours and easy work. In 1943, William, who had become terribly discouraged, sold everything, and he and Miriam took up residence at the Tenant House at Burleigh Manor, where his last son, Davis Monroe, was born.

In the home's listing in the *Maryland Inventory of Historic Properties*, John Monroe Gerwig, the great-grandson of Jacob Frederick Gerwig Sr., is quoted as saying:

> *None in the Gerwig families were heroes, nor financially rich. They claimed no kin to aristocracy. But neither have any been charged as criminals, deserters nor traitors. They were diligent, hard-working, religious, courageous people; leading clean lives and overcoming many untold hardships. They asked no favors from federal, state, and local governments, but paid their taxes and met all obligations when due. Our old house and farm were a bulwark for all of us and we loved them. Our parents and ancestors never would have sold our home. I remember how they sacrificed to preserve it for us children.*

Although family recollections say William Gerwig sold out in 1943, records show that he and his wife, Miriam, sold at least part of the property to Hillie James and Louise Elizabeth McCaliester on July 27, 1938. Hillie, who had come from South Carolina, worked at the Doughnut Corp of America in Ellicott City. Later owners included Joseph W. and Louise German. They sold the property to local high-school sports hero Shirly Leonard Graham and his wife, Grace Porter Graham, on September 28, 1973.

Aerial maps of the property between 1943 and the 1970s show the bulk of the old Gerwig property as vacant save for some homes that were built to the west of the house along Frederick Road, so at some point portions of the original one-hundred-acre farm were sold off.

The Grahams sold the property to Stephen Francis Lintner, twenty-six, and his wife, Paulette Elaine, thirty-four, on April 7, 1977. The couple had gotten married a little over a month earlier in a civil ceremony in Reno, Nevada, on March 3, presumably during a whirlwind, romantic Las Vegas getaway.

At the time, Stephen was a U.S. State Department employee. He, Paulette, her teenaged son Christopher B. Archer from her previous marriage and their dog Emerson moved into the nearly 150-year old house they planned to renovate into their dream home.

Accounts from the Gerwig family describe the house as being in fairly rough condition when the property had passed out of family hands in the late 1930s and early 1940s. Based on the descriptions of the home improvement projects detailed in the 1978 *Maryland Inventory of Historic Properties* report done on the house, the newlyweds had done a great deal of restoration work and had plenty more to do.

Just about every part of the house was taken apart and put back together with loving care. They removed the 1937 bay window on the first-floor west side of the house to create a library nook with floor-to-ceiling bookshelves. In the stone section of the house, the Lintners removed room partitions to create one large light-flooded room with the central fireplace set into the south wall. They also uncovered a charming brick cooking fireplace in the west room of the frame part of the house, as well as the original five-and-three-sixths-inch pine floorboards and a portion of the chair rail that Mrs. Lintner had reproduced and installed in the room. She also added a period-appropriate gold-stencil border around the top of the room. Further stenciling accented the stairways from the first to the second floor and up into the attic and created a border in the southeast bedroom that featured a heart motif.

The couple built a staircase that ran east to west on the south wall of the frame part of the house that led up to two large bedrooms and a large bath over the stone first floor. All of the rooms were painted in colors that were specially mixed by Mrs. Lintner to match Colonial Williamsburg hues.

It was a labor of love that came to a tragic end on the evening of November 22, 1980.

Stephen Lintner was away on an overseas State Department mission, and their son Christopher was gone for the weekend. Paulette Lintner was alone in the house with Emerson that Saturday night when two men broke into her home.

According to an article in the May 29, 1981 issue of the *Baltimore Sun*, Dean Hugh Oliver, twenty-three, and Emerson Anthony Baxter, nineteen, spent the earlier part of that evening drinking, smoking marijuana and visiting friends before deciding to find a home to burglarize. After stealing a truck from the Baltimore janitorial company where Baxter worked, they headed west on Route 40 toward Centennial Lane and pulled into the driveway of the Lintner home.

After picking up a bike and tossing it into the truck, Baxter told the court during his trial, he climbed through an open window and let Oliver in through the kitchen door. He then went upstairs and found a television set that he was in the process of carrying down the stairs when he heard Oliver asking a woman where her money was and the woman saying, "Please don't hurt me." Baxter said she was lying on the kitchen floor and Oliver was stabbing her. He claimed he tried to get the knife away from Oliver. And then the two men fled into the night.

Howard County officer Robert Pollhammer came across the abandoned, disabled truck a few hours later. He opened the door and saw a woman's purse lying on the seat. Inside was a membership card from the Howard County Historical Society. The name on the card read Paulette E. Lintner.

In addition to the purse and the card, the officer found a television, a portable radio, a man's bicycle and a sewing machine, as well as assorted silverware. About two hours later, after repeatedly trying to contact Mrs. Lintner by phone, he drove to the house at 10101 Frederick Road, arriving at approximately 6:00 a.m.

Getting out of his car, he noticed a trail of bloody footprints leading from an open side door, where he saw a woman's legs splayed out on the kitchen floor. He entered the house and came upon an angry, barking dog guarding a woman lying in a pool of blood. It was a crime scene that would haunt Officer Pollhammer for the rest of his life and shake the Ellicott City community to its core.

According to an article in the April 29, 1981 *Baltimore Sun*, the officer's court testimony detailed what he saw. "Inside, he and his lieutenant found Paulette Lintner with her wrists bound by a telephone cord that was looped around her neck, with two knives and a garden rake beside her. She was beaten and her neck was slashed and they believed her dead—until she opened her eyes and attempted to speak."

Baxter and Oliver were arrested within days. They were both charged with murder in the first degree and felony murder, robbery with a deadly weapon, robbery, attempted rape in the first degree, first-degree sexual offense, breaking and entering at night with the intent to commit a felony and intent to steal, theft of less than $300 and assault and battery.

During the course of the investigation, it's reported that before Mrs. Lintner entered the kitchen to investigate the noises she heard, she called out to her dog, saying, "Emerson…is that you?" Baxter, whose first name is Emerson, may have thought she knew him.

Although the state sought to have the two men put to death in the gas chamber, the jury gave them life terms for the murder. As of this writing, Dean Oliver remains behind bars at the maximum-security Western Correctional Institution in Cumberland, Maryland, while Emerson Baxter is serving his life term at the maximum-security Jessup Correctional Facility in Jessup, Maryland.

Paulette was buried at Green Memorial Park, Camp Hill, Pennsylvania, near where she was born and spent the earlier part of her life. Stephen remained in Ellicott City. Despite the horrific tragedy, Stephen continued to live, at least for a few years, in the restored farmhouse that they both had hoped would be their forever home.

A few years later, Stephen, who had earned a PhD in geography and environmental engineering from Johns Hopkins University, found love again and married fellow academic Pamela R. Johnson. On November 19, 1986, just shy of six years to the day Paulette was murdered, Stephen and his new wife sold what had become known as the Gerwig-Lintner House to La Petite Academy, a national daycare company, for $215,000.

Lintner left Ellicott City to take a prestigious job at the World Bank. The couple lived in Washington, D.C., and around 2018 purchased a one-bedroom apartment in the Hotel Des Artistes that had once belonged to 1920s silent-screen star Rudolph Valentino. Their son Christopher remains living in the Baltimore-Washington metro area.

It should come as no surprise that La Petite Academy didn't purchase the Gerwig-Lintner property for its historic and aesthetic value. It promptly bulldozed the beautiful home with the tragic past to build a 6,840-square-foot daycare center on the site. In 1988, La Petite Academy sold .8912 acres of the property to the firm's parent company RIC 24 Ltd. for $801,000. What was left of the Gerwig's 100-acre farm became a housing development in the 1990s.

Bulldozers may have torn down and scraped away the earthly evidence of the Gerwig-Lintner House that stood for 158 years, but there are some things that can't be gotten rid of by carting them off to a landfill. Some things can often only be glimpsed out of the corner of your eye, heard whispered late at night or just sensed in a way that can't be explained. They can remain forever.

# THE HAUNTING

With a property as old as the 1830 Gerwig-Lintner House and a history that goes back to the Carrolls and beyond to the Native Americans who inhabited the area, many people likely died and were buried there over the centuries.

When the Gerwigs first purchased their property, they may not have had the means to bury their dead—including the three first-generation children who didn't make it into adulthood—anywhere but their own backyard.

There is little doubt that most of the Gerwigs who died in the nineteenth century passed away at the house. That, compounded by the death of Paulette Lintner at that same place, may explain the strange occurrences that have been experienced in the daycare center building that was erected on the grave of the Gerwig-Lintner House in 1988.

You couldn't be faulted if you thought any ghostly manifestations on the site of the brutal murder of Paulette Lintner would be very intense and dramatic. But the dead have their own ways.

If the presence some have sensed at the La Petite Academy daycare facility is Mrs. Lintner, she makes herself known only at night after all the toddlers and preschoolers have been picked and most of the staff has gone home. Some, like the lead infant teacher who spent more than sixteen years at the center beginning in the 1990s, soon after the Lintner house was bulldozed, have tales to tell. During her time there, she and many of her colleagues continuously heard and observed disturbing phenomena that can't be easily explained away. They referred to the ghost as "Martha."

A perfectionist about keeping her room tidy and neat, this longtime teacher often stayed late after the center closed in order to put toys and materials away. Most frequently when she knew she was alone there at night, she heard footsteps. It sounded like someone was walking down the hall toward her room. The first few times she heard them, she got up to find out who might be in the building, but no one was there. After that, she noticed the phenomenon but continued about her work.

Another time, a pair of scissors that she had placed on a counter before she went to the supply hallway were gone when she returned. Shortly afterward, she found them on the floor—on the other side of the room.

Then there was the knocking she often heard on her room's closed door. They weren't random sounds. She described them as very purposeful, "like the code knock that people use when they know the person inside." Again, she checked to see who was there the first few times she heard it. Then she simply accepted the "code knock" as whatever spirit was present simply letting her know that it was there.

Perhaps the most unnerving indication that something or somebody not of this world was haunting the halls of the daycare center was what happened with the "clown doll."

The doll sat on a swing hanging over the changing table to entertain children who looked up at it while their diapers were being changed. During the day, it faced outward, looking into the room. But every day, not just once or occasionally when the staff opened the room, they'd find the "clown doll" inexplicably turned backward facing the wall.

"It was freaky. I hated that doll," the teacher recalled.

Over the years, many other employees had similar experiences of objects mysteriously disappearing and reappearing somewhere else and hearing sounds that couldn't be explained. One even claimed to have witnessed the materialized specter walking by them and disappearing into a wall.

Today, as the tides of time have rolled on, decades past the night Paulette Lintner was attacked and spent her last moments looking up at the ceiling of the pretty kitchen of her restored home, it seems that her spirit may have remained. Regardless of whether you believe in ghosts or not, it would be hard not to think that Mrs. Lintner was not ready to leave her beautiful home and the life she loved on that bitter-cold night in November 1980.

# 11

# THE GRAYHOUSE

## GLENWOOD

*A restless ghost rearranges furniture until she is reunited with a long-ago illicit lover.*

Long known as the "Grayhouse behind the Smithy" when a blacksmith shop stood between the home and the road, the dwelling that is now known simply as the Grayhouse is located at 2750 on Route 97. Neat as a pin and exceptionally well-tended by its current owners, this charming, brace-framed, shingled home seems to have been a secondary dwelling to the much better known George W. Powers home, which burned in 2010 and was demolished in 2011. Despite its lesser historical standing, the Grayhouse harbors a significant secret of love and loss that stretches across the sea and eternity.

## THE HISTORY

Like most of the property in and around Glenwood, the land grant the Grayhouse stands on was part of the vast Bushy Park plantation owned by Alexander Warfield. The portion that the house is sited on, along with the blacksmith shop that is shown on the 1860 Martenet map of Howard County, had evidently been handed down to Charles D. Warfield. In 1861, Charles sliced and diced part of the property into ownership with Dr. Evan Warfield and his wife, Sally Ann. Legend has it that around that time, Jeb

George W. Powers (*center in apron*) at his "smithy" in front of the Grayhouse. *Collection of Harvey Goolsby.*

Stuart stole two horses from the Grayhouse property on the way to the Battle of Gettysburg in 1863.

In 1866, a year after the Civil War ended, a total of 438 acres of land grants known as the "Dependence Justifiable" and "Ridgely's Great Park" passed out of Warfield family hands. The property was sold for $18,000 to Aaron Chadwick, thirty, and Emma W. Chadwick, twenty-three, and Aaron's parents, John and Anna Chadwick, all originally from Schenectady, New York. The construction of Grayhouse is said to date from 1840, so it, along with the "smithy" and other buildings, was likely part of the purchase.

The 1870 U.S. Census shows that Aaron and Emma's son Clarence was born around the time the family bought the property. The census also reports that the Chadwicks were farming the land with the help of twenty-two-year-old Black live-in laborer Peregrin "Perry" Dorsey, the son of Soloman and Harriet Dorsey of Lisbon. The Chadwicks also had two "mulatto" servants, Edwin (Edward) Cushion Bond, fourteen, and Fanny Parker, seventeen.

Less than ten years after the Chadwicks purchased the sprawling property, the family turned a tidy profit by selling a little over three acres, including the blacksmith shop and at least two dwellings. On January 1, 1874, blacksmith George W. Powers and his wife, Charity, bought the homestead and the business for $10,000.

The Powers family settled in to live and work in their blacksmith shop on the property. The 1880 U.S. Census shows George (fifty-six) and his wife, Charity (fifty-five), living there with their daughter Laura (twenty-five); son George Oliver (twenty-three), who was also a blacksmith; George's mother, Catherine (seventy-four); his widowed daughter Mary. L. Duvall (twenty-eight); and her son James (nine).

In 1881, George Oliver married Sarah Ann Groomes. They had a son, Edgar C. Powers, in 1883. Instead of following the family trade of blacksmithing, Edgar became a Methodist minister.

The property was subdivided by George Powers's will of 1894 and given to his children after his death in 1905. George Oliver and his wife received the Grayhouse and the smithy shops. His daughters Mary E. Duval and Laura V. Powers got their father's house, which has since burned. Both bequests were conditioned on the children continuing to support their mother, Charity, who departed this life in 1913.

In July 1933, George Oliver and Sarah A. Powers conveyed the Grayhouse and shops to Mary Koontz, who turned around and sold the property to Edgar C. and Sarah A. Powers on the same day. Less than ten years later, Sarah passed away, in 1942, and George Oliver followed her to the grave in Oak Grove Cemetery in 1945.

Edgar then sold the property to Earl Eugene and Alice Elizabeth Walker. Besides the house and buildings, the only reminder of the Powers family is a stone marked "G.W.P." that remains to this day in the back paddock

The Walkers moved in with their sons, nine-year-old Earl and Millard, who was born that same year. Earl later worked as a truck driver at Tidewater Express in Baltimore. The Walkers lived there until October 15, 1952, when they sold the property to Jesse Franklin Hakes and Mary Wilson Mish Hakes.

The Hakes were quite wealthy and didn't live on the Powers property. They made their home across the street at Ellerslie Plantation, a grand manor house dating to 1783 sited on a total of three hundred acres that they had purchased in 1945. Although the M.I.T.-educated Jesse Hakes was the inventor of the "star drill" and founder of Baltimore Tool Works, it seems that gardening was his and his wife's true passion. While no confirming documentation was found, Hakes is said to have been a fellow of the Royal Society of Horticulturalists and to have developed a variety of blue rhododendron dubbed "Mrs. Hakes" that graced Ellerslie's extensive gardens.

In 1973, the Hakes sold both of the Powers properties. Architect Harvey Wilson Goolsby III and his wife, Sandra Ann Bridges Goolsby, who had been eyeing up property in the area for years, paid $100 to be the first to see both the Grayhouse and the George W. Powers house.

As other potential buyers sat honking their horns in the driveway, the Goolsbys decided that the Grayhouse was the one they wanted. On May 31, they bought the 1,822-square-foot home on 1.625 acres for the full asking price of $34,000 and moved in on June 15.

When the Goolsbys told their Howard County friends about their purchase and gave a description of where it was, the response was always, "Oh! Emma's house." The Emma they were referring to was Emma (Warfield/ Gramkow) McCormack, who had rented the house from the Hakes and lived there for fourteen years.

Born in 1899, Emma was the daughter of Governor Edwin Warfield and a cousin of the notorious Wallis Warfield Simpson. She married Frank Elmer Gramkow of Wellesley, Massachusetts, and had a son, Edwin, in 1926.

When Frank died in 1948, Emma came back home to Howard County, where she was a very social and popular figure. She was fond of entertaining guests at the Grayhouse in what was known as "the coldest kitchen in the county." It's said that she and her friends "polished off many a bottle of bourbon" there. Emma later moved to a house on the grounds of the Warfield manor home at Oakdale, where she died in 1971.

Soon after the Goolsbys bought "Emma's house," the strange occurrences began.

Although the dwelling was built nearly two hundred years ago and was home to at least three family owners, a handful of enslaved people and servants, as well as what was probably a smattering of renters over the years, it seems that only one of them stayed to haunt the house.

## THE HAUNTING

Compact but elegant, with gracious proportions, the Grayhouse couldn't be a prettier place for a haunting. Set upon a rise on the western side of Route 97, it has lovely views out of almost every window.

The parlor that spans the southern side of the home with its welcoming fireplace and high ceilings was the perfect place for the Goolsbys to relax and unwind with their two young sons, Kirk and Crispin.

Except that, for a long time, it wasn't.

At the time they moved in, both Harvey and Sandy worked in Baltimore while their youngest son was taken care of by a babysitter and their older one attended kindergarten.

Nobody was home at the Grayhouse during the day.

Yet most every evening, when the family returned home, Harvey and Sandy noticed that the furniture in the parlor was slightly rearranged.

Chairs that had been positioned at the eastern and western ends of the room were drawn in closer to face each other in front of the fireplace, as if unseen visitors wanted to warm themselves as they chatted about ghostly matters. Something or someone also regularly slid the sofa, which was situated directly across from the fireplace, toward the door at the eastern end of the room.

At first, questions flew between the couple. "Did you move the chairs?" "Why did you push the sofa down the wall?" But, of course, neither of them had done it.

After a while, they just shrugged and moved the furniture back into place every night. They came to refer to whatever or whoever was doing it as "our poltergeist." And as a nod to the home's most beloved past tenant, the Goolsbys playfully called the ghost "Emma."

They gave little thought to the motivations of their unseen furniture-rearranger until one cold winter day in November 1975.

One of the primary reasons the Goolsbys had moved to the country was Harvey's interest in hunting. Within two weeks of moving into the Grayhouse, he had bought a Thoroughbred hunter horse and began going out riding with the Howard County Hounds.

One cold Saturday, there was a "hunt breakfast" at the old Hunt Club property on Tridelphia Road in the late afternoon after the hounds had been brought in. The room had been set up with big round tables that seated eight or so people. Harvey came to be seated at a table that included someone new: a very handsome woman named Melissa "Missy" Constant.

The daughter of Alfred Warfield, Missy was at that time in the final stages of a divorce and had come home to live in one of the Warfield family's many homes and to help her parents.

Conversation among people who follow hounds is easy. Having shared the risks and travails of that day's long, cold hunt, Harvey's talk with Missy covered a range of topics. In the course of their chat, he learned that the "Emma" who had lived at the Grayhouse had been Missy's late aunt. Harvey proceeded to tell her the story of the Grayhouse's poltergeist, which they

Thoughtfully updated and meticulously maintained, the Grayhouse has aged very gracefully. *Harvey Goolsby*.

had named after her. It was a tale that was good for winter laughs over warm food and spirits.

Only later in the afternoon, as the day was turning into evening, did Harvey go on to relate a story—and hear one—that would stun them both.

Over the summer and into the fall, Harvey and Sandy became uncommonly concerned with what had become headline news of the day: the long-suffering, sporadic recoveries and the slow death of Generalissimo Francisco Franco, who had led the fight to overthrow the government and ruled as dictator over Spain from 1939 to 1975.

In relating the story to Missy, Harvey admitted that this was a little odd, since neither he nor his wife were fans of Franco or sympathizers with the Caudillo's policies or politics. But for some reason, it had been on their mind.

And then he said something that stopped the conversation in its tracks.

"Funny thing," Harvey said, "all of 'Emma's' furniture-rearranging activities stopped in November, about the time that we heard that Franco died."

At that point, Missy's jaw dropped and all the color drained from her face. "It stopped when Franco died?" she whispered.

Missy went on to relate a story that made the hairs stand up on the back of Harvey's neck.

It seems that, in 1936, Emma was living in Spain with her ten-year-old son, Edwin. In the middle of the night on July 17, she was awakened by the sound of soldiers banging on the door. They rousted Emma, her son and a servant out of bed and hustled them into a waiting car. From there, they sped off to the coast.

There, high-ranking military officers put the trio on a ship that quickly left the harbor and headed for Le Havre, France, escorted by six gunboats, which at that time would have constituted approximately one-quarter of the Spanish navy.

Once safely in France, they were put up in a luxurious inn. It turns out that Emma and her son had been spirited out of the country just hours before the violent start of the Spanish Civil War.

But by whom?

The Warfield family had always suspected but never knew for sure that Emma had an affair while she was in Spain. Her story of the midnight escape to France confirmed their long-held suspicions that her lover had been none other than Generalissimo Francisco Franco Bahamonde.

The connection between the ghostly manifestations and their cessation at the Grayhouse was now clear.

Some essence of Emma must have returned to the house after her death in 1971 to sit in front of a long-extinguished fire with dearly departed friends, night after night, in the parlor, waiting for the day four years later when her handsome Spanish lover could return to her arms in the world beyond this one.

After Emma and Franco were reunited in the next world, the furniture in the Grayhouse never moved again.

# 12

# SUNNYSIDE

## LISBON

*The Warfield dead slumber elsewhere,*
*but their ever-watchful spirits remain at home.*

The wide-open expanses of farmland in western Howard County that are now slowly being filled up with new development used to be home to a tight-knit network of a handful of interrelated old Howard County families. There were few more storied or accomplished than the Warfields.

In addition to their original family home at Cherry Grove, the Warfields built the stately mansion at Oakdale, home of Maryland governor Edwin Warfield. Next to Wallis Simpson Warfield, the governor was the most famous of them all. But not every home of even the most prominent family is well known.

Such is the case of Sunnyside. Located near Lisbon, at what was 2598 Route 94, now recorded as 2701 Woodbine Road, this often-overlooked historic home harbors good-hearted spirits that have entertained children, averted disasters and offered to continue to serve the Warfields who lived there.

# THE HISTORY

When it was first built, the architecturally eclectic home known as Sunnyside was little more than a shelter from the elements, as were many of even some of the most impressive historic homes in Howard County. It started out as a simple log house built by Joshua Warfield on part of the 590 acres of land called "Fredericksburg" that his father, Captain Benjamin Warfield, had purchased from Henry Griffith in 1766.

Located less than two miles from Cherry Grove, the original part of this 1768 Warfield family house was a two-bay-wide, one-room-deep, two-story-high structure that rests on a stone foundation and features a square, brick chimney on its south wall. Although Joshua built the log home, family members say he never lived there, but rather inherited Cherry Grove and stayed on after his father died in 1807.

Even though Jacob may have never lived at the house, the history of Sunnyside is closely entwined with that of this branch of the Warfield family. In 1812, thirty-one-year-old Joshua married Rachel Griffith Welsh, the daughter of Samuel and Rachel Welsh. The couple had two children together, Avolina, born in 1813, and Nicolas Ridgely, born in 1815.

Sadly, Rachel passed away on February 27, 1816, at the age of thirty, leaving Joshua with their two toddlers. Joshua wasted very little time getting on with his life. He rather quickly married Lydia Dorsey Welsh, twenty-six, the daughter of John and Lucretia Dorsey Welsh, on March 12, 1816. Lydia bore two children, Albert Gallatin Warfield in 1817, followed by Catherine Dorsey Warfield in 1818.

It's said that it was the first Albert Gallatin who build the L-shaped center section of Sunnyside in 1830. This two-story addition features a wide, corbeled brick south chimney as well as a two-story-high, shed-roofed open porch that runs along the east side of the house.

Like his father, however, Albert never lived at Sunnyside. He and his wife, Margaret Gassaway Watkins, instead resided at the elegant and impressive Oakdale manor, which he built in 1838. There, he and Margaret raised ten children, including a future governor of Maryland, Edwin Warfield.

The next chapter of the history belongs to Albert and Margaret's second son, Joshua Nicholas, born at Oakdale in 1845. In 1880, Joshua married Lucy W. Hutton and moved to Sunnyside. There at the property that his father had given him, he and Lucy raised three children: Joshua Nicholas Warfield Jr., born in 1884; Margaret G. Warfield, born in 1885; and Norman Hutton Warfield, born on March 7, 1889.

Added on to and remodeled many times, Sunnyside is a treasure box filled with secrets. *Maryland Historical Trust.*

Described by family members as a "wheeler-dealer," Joshua was a big, robust man who was said to have had an ability to "buy and sell" to his advantage. A real estate appraiser by trade, he formed his own title company to facilitate his various land purchases. But buying land wasn't his only interest. As an organic gardener long before it became fashionable, Joshua contracted with a company in Washington, D.C., to collect waste and garbage, which he composted to fertilize the fields at Sunnyside and his tenant farm.

To make room for his growing family, Joshua added a third story to the house and a three-story, shingled front section to Sunnyside in 1890. This addition created a large, central entrance hall flanked by a dining room and family room leading back to the original staircase. It's said that his son Norman later added a front porch.

By the end of the nineteenth century, Sunnyside was completed. The additions and modifications created during the course of nearly 150 years resulted in what has been described as an "interesting" living space that subsequent owners continued to tinker with during the twentieth century.

Joshua Sr. departed this life on August 19, 1919, and his son Norman Hutton and Norman's wife, Clara Warfield—a daughter of another branch of the Warfield family—took possession of Sunnyside. Norman's mother must have moved away from Sunnyside shortly after her husband's death, as the U.S. Census of 1920 shows sixty-two-year-old Lucy Warfield living with her son Joshua Jr. and his wife, Mary, in a house "south of Frederick Turnpike." Lucy followed her husband to the grave in 1927. Like her husband and generations before them, she was buried in the Warfield Family Cemetery.

Meanwhile, back at Sunnyside, Norman and Clara settled into the old family homestead. Together, they spent almost thirty-five years there. Norman worked the land and pursued business interests while Clara took care of maintaining the lovely home and entertaining their wide circle of family and friends.

Their lives were pleasant but not terribly long. Clara passed away first, at the age of sixty-four, on April 1, 1954. Norman followed her to the grave a little more than two years later. He died at the age of sixty-six at Union Memorial Hospital on May 2, 1955, after a three-week illness. In addition to maintaining what was then the five-hundred-acre farm, Norman served as president of the Howard County School Board and had been the chief appraiser and an officer of the Federal Land Bank of Baltimore. He also served as a director and board member of several local banks.

Norman and Clara had no children. So, early in 1955, Norman drew up a last will and testament that bequeathed 302.877 acres and Sunnyside to his ten-year-old cousin Albert Gallatin Warfield III. It was to be held in trust until little "Gally" reached the age of thirty.

At the time, Gally and his family were living at Wakefield Farm, a Warfield family property just across the road of the back entrance to the Oakdale estate. It was the home of his grandfather Marshall Turrene Warfield Sr., the youngest son of Albert Gallatin Warfield I and his much younger wife, Lucy W. Holland Warfield.

Marshall Sr. and Lucy had two sons, Albert Gallatin Warfield II and Marshall Turrene Warfield Jr. Marshall Sr., who passed away in 1929, didn't live to see the accomplishments of both sons or the tragic death of Marshall, who served in the army in World War II as a first lieutenant and was killed on September 17, 1944, at the Battle of Metz in Nievre, Bourgogne, France. Four years later, after the war ended, his body was recovered and buried at the Warfield Family Cemetery in Woodbine.

Albert enlisted in 1941 and enrolled in Infantry Training School. During the course of the war, he rose to the rank of lieutenant colonel and earned a Bronze Star with Oakleaf Cluster, a Silver Star and the Distinguished

Service Order from the King of England. He was fortunate enough to survive the war and return to his wife, Caroline Garner Kirwan Warfield, whom he had married in 1941.

After Norman passed away, Gally and his parents, along with his sisters Mary Hutton "Missy" and Caroline, took up residence at Sunnyside in 1956. There, in addition to serving as lord of the Sunnyside manor, Albert Sr. was a partner and manager of the Baltimore office of Pierce, Fenner and Smith Inc.

As accomplished as it was, the professional life of Gally's father, Albert, was arguably eclipsed in terms of being interesting by the career of his mother, Caroline. Born in Bolton Hill in Baltimore, she attended the Maryland Institute College of Art and moved to New York City in the 1930s, joining the staff of the *News-Post* and writinge feature stories under the byline Caroline Kirwan.

Gally's sister Mary Hutton "Missy" Warfield Hollingsworth described her mother in Caroline's 2002 *Baltimore Sun* obituary as "an independent cuss" and "a man's woman, not a woman's woman."

By all accounts, Mrs. Warfield was an imposing woman. She stood five feet, eight inches tall, was a striking presence with her dark hair and eyes and smooth complexion. Her daughter went on to say that her mother "was big-boned, always wore red, red lipstick, and had kind of a Lauren Bacall look about her."

She died in 2002 at Fairhaven Nursing Home in Sykesville at the age of ninety-one. Her memorial service was held at Sunnyside. Afterward, she was buried at the family cemetery alongside her husband, Albert, who had passed away on April 19, 1983.

Before they died, both of Gally's parents lived to see the day on August 25, 1976, when he came into his inheritance and took possession of Sunnyside. At the time, he was serving as the assistant state's attorney for Howard County. Shortly thereafter, he married Marsha "Misty" Ann Smith, a local girl from Ellicott City.

Together, they welcomed twins, a boy, Albert Gallatin IV, and a girl, Erin, to what seemed like the never-ending line of Warfield descendants who would always call Sunnyside their home. Sadly, the marriage ended in 1987, but the couple's relationship with the historic house continued. Gally stayed at Sunnyside and shared custody of the girls with Misty, who moved to a house a short distance away.

In 1978, the property was added to the *Maryland Inventory of Historic Properties*. Modified, improved and updated many times over its then nearly

150-year history, the home was described as featuring a wide variety of interesting and unique details.

The original log house, which had been turned into a separate apartment, still had its random-width floors and massive stone fireplace with original iron cooking crane. The apartment was connected to the main house by a passage containing a dumb waiter that brought food prepared downstairs up to the first floor. Originally, Sunnyside had an enclosed stairway along the north wall. It was subsequently replaced by a modern circular staircase that now leads from the first to the third floors.

In 1979, Warfield took steps to preserve and protect the home and farm by selling development rights on 230 acres of the 400-plus-acre property for $298,850 to the newly formed Maryland Agricultural Land Preservation Foundation.

Twenty years later, more than 232 years of the Warfield family's ownership of the Sunnyside part of the Fredericksburg land grant that Benjamin Warfield purchased in 1766 came to an end. Warfield sold Sunnyside, on 193.58 acres, to Robert P. Long Jr. and Leslie P. Long for $1,100,000. The couple transformed the property into a Thoroughbred breeding farm, freeing Gally to pursue a career writing books and screenplays in Hollywood.

So, on a fine spring day in May 1998, Albert Gallatin Warfield III, the last living Warfield owner of Sunnyside, walked out of the log cabin that became one of the grandest homes in Howard County, leaving only echoes of his footsteps and, perhaps, the spiritual remnants of those who came before.

## THE HAUNTING

Although Sunnyside has stood down a long lane off Woodbine Road for more than two hundred years, the members of the Warfield family who lived and died there didn't stick around. At least their mortal remains didn't.

Unlike many of the Howard County homesteads of the time, Sunnyside has no family graveyard on the property. While it's likely that many of the enslaved people who lived and worked on the farm are interred there in graves that may have been marked only by wooden signs that have long since crumbled into dust, the bodies of generations of Warfield fathers, mothers and children were ferried down the road in grand style to their final resting place in the family cemetery at Cherry Grove.

Although none of them are buried at Sunnyside, it seems many of their spirits remained behind at the grand old home. Some say—and have seen—the Warfield family spirits that still roam the halls of the great home and its gently rolling property. Although it's been nearly a quarter of a century since the last Warfield walked its floorboards, the home is remembered as the site of a variety of strange happenings by those who lived and spent time there. Among the most unnerving involves the old arch-topped toy chest on the third floor.

The young great-great-great-granddaughter and grandson of Joshua Warfield discovered it in the early 1980s. Exploring the house, they climbed up the tall circular stairway to the top floor of the house, where they came upon the dust-covered wooden box. Opening it, they were delighted to discover all kinds of wonderful old toys that had remained neatly arranged in their places for decades if not a century or more.

They pulled them out one by one and began having fun with the dolls, blocks, tops and other old-fashioned playthings. Lost in their games, hours passed until they heard someone calling them down to dinner. They hurriedly stuffed the toys back into the chest and pushed it into its original place.

The next day, remembering all the fun they'd had the afternoon before, the twins ran up the three flights of stairs to continue their games. The chest was still there where they had left it. But although they were sure they'd closed it up tight the night before, they looked at it in surprise. The lid of the toy chest was wide open.

When they saw what was inside, they stopped in their tracks.

The toys that they had hastily tossed into the chest were all lined up, carefully placed back in the orderly arrangement they had found the day before. Although the children were startled, the feeling of the family was that it was the ghost of a very organized Warfield child from long ago that had come back to put her things in their rightful place.

Whoever the spirits in the house were, they seemed to be benevolent. It was as if the Warfield dead were watching over and protecting their living descendants. There were frequent sounds of furniture being moved around in other rooms. The family exchanged knowing looks but mostly ignored the sounds. Specters appeared to the children on the stairs. Once, one of the ghosts—that of a man, they think—was more overt in protecting the family.

One night, unbeknownst to the family, a storm was blowing up in the distance. Shortly before it hit, an outdoor spotlight began turning off and on, alerting them to the coming windstorm and giving them time to secure the outdoor furniture.

Now, a large home, built in the early nineteenth century by one of the prominent families in the county, undoubtedly had many enslaved people working and living on the property. They most likely would have been buried there when they died.

Long after emancipation, African Americans continued to work at Sunnyside. The 1920 U.S. Census lists Mary Boswell, fifty-nine, and Joseph Lightfoot, nineteen, living at the home as servants to Norman and Clara Warfield. Their lives of hard work and service—and those who came before them—may have included a fondness for the home and a sense of devotion to the people who lived there—a love that perhaps caused them to linger long after their deaths.

Here is the story of what may be one of those departed servants, in the words of Misty Ann Warfield shared in an interview with the author.

> *There is an incident that I have pondered throughout the years that happened in that same time frame of the late seventies. I don't know if what I saw was a spirit or a living being; but, thinking of it in hindsight, it was very odd. We had had a party that went on late into the night, an outdoor party in the summer. It was the next morning, and I was outside looking at all of the tables and a post-party mess to be cleaned up.*
>
> *Suddenly, across the yard, maybe forty yards away standing under some trees, I saw a young Black man, maybe late twenties, wearing a dark-colored suit and a white shirt with the suit jacket unbuttoned. The suit was old-fashioned-looking; plain and simple. I vaguely remember he was wearing an old-fashioned hat, like one of those porkpie ones, I think they are called.*
>
> *He called out to me, asking if I needed help cleaning up, and I said "no." Then he was gone. I don't remember him walking away. It was odd, because Sunnyside was an expansive property with very long back and front lanes and I had never seen anyone like that on the property before or since. Lisbon at that time was not like it is now with all of the development, just large farms and smaller houses and you didn't see people walking the roads or roaming around or trespassing on private property. I still don't know if it was a living being or a ghost that showed up that day.*

Far from being scary, the ghosts of Sunnyside seem to be keeping watch over their old home and the family they never knew in life but perhaps will be reunited with in death.

# 13

# ROXBURY

## GLENELG

*A haunted homestead crumbles in the face of tragic deaths,*
*a crushing curse and the onslaught of time.*

Set well back off the south side of an old byway, the home most recently known as Roxbury was once located at 15085 Roxbury Road. The lovely brick, frame and stone house, as well as the farm buildings, were set amid rolling fields, with the home on the east side of the drive and most of the farm buildings to the west. It was home to three generations of Clarks, a wealthy Washington, D.C. lawyer, a financier and his socialite wife and, finally, a humble tenant farmer who poured his savings, love and life into a farm where spirits roamed and memory alone now reigns.

## THE HISTORY

Known alternatively as the Clark Family House and the George Chase Brick House, Roxbury stood on acreage that was part of the "Friendship," "Vanity Mount" and the "Sapling Range" land grant patented in 1744 by Henry Ridgely and that passed into the hands of the Dorsey and Owings families.

In 1841, the property was owned by Charles Ridgely Simpson and his wife, Sarah Ann Dorsey. That year, they sold two tracts of land totaling 137 acres near Roxbury Mill to David Clark Jr. and his wife, Rachel Maria Dorsey.

David was the son of David Clark Sr., one of three Clark brothers who immigrated to Anne Arundel County from Northern Ireland just after the American Revolution and founded a wool carding mill. A farmer by trade, Clark Jr. also served as a county commissioner from 1851 to 1853.

There may have been rudimentary buildings on the property when David and Rachel bought Roxbury. In 1861, the transfer book assessed Clark Jr. $700 for a "new house" that was cobbled together from re-used material.

That may explain the brick-and-frame home's unusual floor plan. It featured a central vestibule with an enclosed stairway and a third room in the center. The stone kitchen wing at the back of the house was likely built before the home's estimated 1860 construction date, perhaps as early as 1774.

The 1860 U.S. Census shows the Clarks living with their sons John Owings (nineteen), James Henry (seventeen) and George Dorsey (fifteen). By then, their three older daughters—Margaretta Elizabeth, Frances Elizabeth and Isabella—were out of the house.

In 1868, George married Alice Ann Linthicum, and they quickly had a daughter, Margaretta, in 1869, and then Florence Amanda a year later. The 1870 U.S. Census says the little family lived at Roxbury with George's parents and his brother James, along with John Willis, Emily Thorn and Benjamin Allen, all African American servants.

Two years later, in 1872, George and Alice had another daughter, Alice Naomi, who sadly didn't live long. The girl left this world in 1878 at the age of six and was buried in the family cemetery on the property.

Their daughter Mary Isabella was born in 1873. George Thomas came along in 1875 and William arrived in 1876. Little Matilda V. was born on August 10, 1886, but lived only seven months. She died on March 7, 1887, and joined her sister in the cemetery where both of their gravestones still stand.

Death continued ruthlessly stalking Roxbury through the waning years of the nineteenth century,

David Clark Jr. died in 1897. At the time of his death, he was in the process of dividing up Roxbury between two of his sons. James received 100 acres. George Dorsey was given 137 acres and the existing buildings.

Tragically, George died just a few years later, on July 18, 1900, at the age of fifty-five. The cause of death was internal injuries caused by a fall while he was stacking wheat in his hay barrack. Records say he languished in pain for two weeks at Roxbury before departing this life

At the time of George's death, the family owned five working horses, one driving horse, seven milk cows, two sows and seventeen shoats. The oats and

Partially bulldozed in 2019, Roxbury remains in the hearts and memories of former owners. *Maryland Historical Trust.*

wheat they grew on the farm were harvested but not threshed. There was a stored crop of hay and corn in the ground.

In addition to the main house, there were numerous outbuildings at Roxbury, including a barn, stable, corn house, henhouse, meat house, tenant house, carriage house and wagon shed.

Alice and the children continued to live at the farm until 1913, when she sold it to her son George Thomas and Sallie M. Clark. Before that, in 1905, Thomas bought an adjoining two-hundred-acre farm at public auction and probably lived there. Alice continued to live at Roxbury until her death on January 11, 1928. After that date, the home may have been used as a tenant house.

In 1949, after nearly one hundred years of Clark family ownership, Thomas sold both farms to George Howland Chase III and his Austrian-born wife, Mary Cameron Hale. A wealthy, Harvard-educated lawyer, George Chase was part of the firm Cravath, de Gersdorff, Swaine & Wood in Washington, D.C., and served as an assistant general counsel of the Federal Reserve Board. Their main residence was in Washington, with Roxbury serving as an investment property and occasional summer weekend retreat.

Five years after the Chases purchased the property, their only daughter, Mary Eugenia Chase Guild, a graduate of Bryn Mawr College and wife of Samuel Eliot Guild Jr., died suddenly on April 20, 1954, at the age of just twenty-three.

The Chases continued to own Roxbury until 1978. Then, having no heirs to leave the property to and being extremely well off, they deeded an easement on the farm to the Maryland Environmental Trust.

Two years later, in 1980, the Chases turned Roxbury over to longtime tenants Charles Gerald and Linda Carole Collins Zepp at no cost, with the understanding that they live on and farm the property in return for paying the taxes.

They and their sons Charles Jr. and William continued to live and work on the property until the Zepps got into financial trouble. They ended up selling Roxbury and its 261.468 acres to Charles A. and Denise D. Sharp, owners of Sharps Waterford Farms, for $694,660 on February 16, 1994.

It's said that Mrs. Sharp had an uneasy feeling about the property and refused to live in the house. Because of that, they allowed the Zepp family to stay on to farm the property as renters. They did so until Charles Sr. died in 1996 and was buried in the Clark family graveyard.

After the Zepp family's departure, the Sharps rented Roxbury out to various tenants. Later, the house stood empty until 2018. That year, their company, Sharps Wild Horse Meadow LLC, sold fifty-one acres to Roxbury View LLC for $2,325,126. After nearly two hundred years, most of the old Clark homestead met its death by bulldozers in 2019 to make way for a subdivision.

By chance or some sense of historical mercy, the stone kitchen wing was left standing. This silent testament to generations of Clarks as well as the Chase and Zepp families is all that remains. However, stories of the spirits that inhabited the property continue to live on in the memories of those who encountered them.

# THE HAUNTING

It's understandable for a house that was home to generations of Clarks who lost their share of family members to disease, tragic accidents and old age to harbor spirits that wanted to stay or couldn't quite make their way to the light. And from stories told by those who lived at Roxbury, there seem to be quite a few flitting around the old homestead while it stood.

But the most disturbing story about Roxbury is perhaps what some have called a curse that descended on the Charles Gerald Zepp Sr. family after he, his wife, Linda, and their two little boys, Charles Jr. and William, moved into Roxbury as tenant farmers in 1970.

The first intimation of the trouble to come may have been in 1973, when Linda Zepp hosted a group of girlfriends and their children at a get-together at Roxbury. The group ended up at the old graveyard where many of the Clarks are buried.

Mysteriously referred to in historical records as the old "Gilpin alias Pressley" reserve family graveyard, the burial ground is surrounded by a concrete block wall and is located in the middle of a large field.

While Linda's fascinated guests were reading the names on the six-inch-thick, three-foot-wide-by-four-foot-high headstones and the children were chasing the family dog around the cemetery, something very strange happened. As the children were racing around the cemetery, one of the gravestones suddenly fell over, crushing little Erik Burdick's foot. Screaming, the women rushed to lift the stone to slide the child's leg out from under a monument that had previously been held up by half an inch of rebar that was now bent over.

After that, no one went back to the cemetery.

According to Charles Zepp Jr., who recounted the incident, they let the toppled stone lay there for years. At some point, the marker was mysteriously placed back upright by an unknown force or person. It's said that the events of that night continue to haunt those who were there and that Erik still has trouble with his foot.

Over the years, there were numerous unexplained incidents inside the house. Radios would mysteriously go off and on. Unplugged televisions continued to broadcast. Charles Sr. reached out to what he thought was his wife but encountered nothing but air. Charles Jr. said the bedroom up the back stairs felt like a very dark and foreboding place.

In 1980, after George Chase granted Roxbury to the Zepp family, the clan rejoiced at their great good fortune. Seeing a bright future ahead, Charles invested most of what they had in a herd of cattle. That hopeful future almost immediately dimmed when the entire herd died of a rare disease.

Undaunted and eternally optimistic, Zepp borrowed money to purchase more cattle. They all died, too. In financial distress, the Zepps had to sell the farm in 1994 but stayed on as renters.

Unfortunately, the curse of Roxbury was not done with the Zepp family. The new owners came over to the farm on Halloween with their son to celebrate the macabre holiday with a bonfire near the graveyard. Their festivities may have conjured more ill will from the spirits at the "Gilpin alias Pressley" reserve family graveyard.

Soon after, Charles Zepp Sr., beaten down by bad luck, heartbreak and perhaps the curse of unsettled ghosts, was stricken with lung cancer. He died on June 24, 1996, at the age of fifty-one.

In accord with his dying wish, Charles joined the departed Clarks in the old graveyard at Roxbury, where his tombstone stands to this day. In death, he became forever a part of the farm that he and his family loved for over twenty-six years.

Hopefully, the names on the grave markers in the cemetery, the ancient hewn granite kitchen wing and Zepp's undying love for the property will keep Roxbury alive in the memories and imagination of the living for generations to come.

# 14

# THE WAYSIDE INN

## ELLICOTT CITY

*A long-dead housekeeper warns of death in elegant chambers
eternally lit by candlelight.*

Before it was hidden from view by a sound barrier wall, even occasional travelers along old Route 29 couldn't help but be captivated by the sight of this stately stone home where every window was illuminated by candles that "burned" around the clock. Constructed in the Quaker style by a prominent Maryland–West Virginia family, the Wayside Inn, located at 4344 Columbia Road, only recently began living up to its name and revealing its ghostly secrets.

## THE HISTORY

The land that the imposing granite home known as the Wayside Inn stands on was part of the 98-acre parcel that was granted to Henry Pierpoint by his Lordships Land Office in 1755. After a survey in 1757, it was patented as "The Search." In 1787, Pierpoint added another 112 acres to his holdings and patented the expanded property as "The Search Enlarged."

Henry and his wife, Rebecca, were Quakers from West River. The refined yet plain granite house they built sometime around 1780 reflects the sensibilities of that faith tradition. Although formal in the Federal style, the

Once a wealthy landowner's home, the Wayside Inn is now a bed-and-breakfast. *Maryland Historical Trust.*

home is very simple inside and out. The rough-finished plaster walls, lack of crown molding and basic mantles and trim are very much in keeping with spare Quaker values. That being said, Quakers were comfortable demonstrating their wealth with the size of their homes. Pierpoint was a man of means, and the enormous scale of his house shows it.

In 1785, three years before his death, Pierpoint sold forty-five acres of "The Search Enlarged" as well as its "premises and appurtenances" to Dr. Michael Pue and his wife, Mary Dorsey Pue. The purchase price was reported to be four pounds sterling an acre, which was a substantial increase over the next-to-nothing one shilling per acre that Pierpoint had paid for it.

Dr. Pue had immigrated to the United States from Dublin, Ireland, in 1770 at the age of twenty-eight. He had married Mary Dorsey of Belmont a year earlier. In 1778, he took the "Oath of Fidelity and Support," swearing allegiance to the state of Maryland and denying allegiance and obedience to Great Britain. It was a required oath during the American Revolutionary War.

The 1790 U.S. Census listed five males, seven females, plus one more free person and nineteen enslaved people living on the property. By that time, the household included the Pues' children: Anne (eighteen), Arthur William (fourteen) and Eleanor (eleven). Their son Edward was born at the house in 1788, followed by Caleb in 1791.

Sadly, Dr. Pue departed this life just four years after Caleb's birth, on July 19, 1795, at the age of just fifty-three. He was buried in the Belmont Manor Cemetery on the grounds of his wife's family home in Elkridge.

That year, the house passed into the hands of their son Arthur William Pue, who had followed his father's career path to become a doctor. Pue and his wife, Rebecca Ridgely, welcomed their son Arthur Jr. to the family in 1804 and Henry Hill in 1810. In 1833, grandmother Mary Dorsey passed away and joined her husband, Michael, and son in the family plot at Belmont.

After his father's death in 1847, Henry Hill Pue inherited the property and quickly sold it to Welsh-born farmer Evan Hughes and his wife, Margaret E., in 1848.

The 1850 U.S. Census shows the Hughes family living at the home with their children—eight-year-old Jane, six-year-old Sarah and two-year-old son Evan—along with two Irish farmhands, Francis O'Neal and Thomas Leach. Another daughter, Isabel, arrived in 1859.

At the time of Evan Hughes's death in 1860, the Martinet map for Howard County shows him owning a total of 265 acres, having purchased the additional land between 1848 and 1858. Margaret stayed on at the house and eventually married James E. Poland in 1867. The 1912 Howard County Directory indicates that the house and land were still owned by the Poland family. It remained an active farm until the 1920s, when they sold it to Morris and Rebecca Shapiro.

Shapiro was the president of C.A. Gambrills Manufacturing Company. He bought, subdivided and sold properties, including the land that St. Charles College on Frederick Road stood on before it burned in 1911. He likely subdivided the Poland farm, selling parcels of it to various buyers. Records show that Edward T. and Alda Hodges Clark were among them, each buying acreage in 1923 and 1930. They, too, probably subdivided the land into lots and sold them, since the present-day neighborhood is called the Edward T. Subdivision.

By 1937, the Wayside Inn was owned by Harry and Abbie Scott Parlett. They seem to have lived there until at least Harry's death in 1952 at the age of eighty-seven. Other owners included Charles and Ruth Hardy. It's said that the property fell into disrepair until Robert and Charlotte Hartkopf, who owned and operated what was then the Cheshire Inn on Baltimore National Parkway, purchased the home in 1963. After renovating it, they applied for and got its first historical designation.

In 1976, the Hartkopfs sold the home to Joseph G. and Cheryl H. Gerard, who in turn sold it to John F. and Margo J. Osantowski on June 5, 1981, for

$170,000. It was the Osantowskis who renovated the third floor and first opened the Wayside Inn as a bed-and-breakfast. In 1998, former McCormick Spice Company executive David Balderson and his wife, Susan, bought the property for $400,000 and took over the reins of the bed-and-breakfast, making significant upgrades and additions to the home.

Twenty years later, the Baldersons were ready to move on. On October 10, 2018, Liu Jinxing of the Wayside Inn of Maryland Inc. purchased the nearly six-thousand-square-foot property on 1.920 acres for $944, 900. Today, the Wayside Inn continues to welcome guests to enjoy its gracious charms and occasional supernatural encounter.

# THE HAUNTING

Clocking in at over 240 years of age, the Wayside Inn has seen a lot of history come and go through its welcoming front door. Local lore claims that both John Adams and George Washington stayed there. No one knows for sure, because there are no records indicating that it was anything more than a private home until the Osandtowskis turned it into a bed-and-breakfast.

However, it's understandable why the legend caught on.

The house fronts what was once the Old Columbia Turnpike, a road that ran only from Ellicott's Mills to Columbia in 1795. The full length of the byway was voted into existence in 1809 by the Maryland legislature to take travelers from Ellicott's Mills to Georgetown. An original milepost still stands about two hundred yards south of the inn with the inscription "2M to E.C."

In addition to the location of the house being a convenient stopping place for travelers, the Pierpoints and Pues were prominent local families. The house is huge, and Howard County welcomes are famously warm. It's not hard to imagine high-profile travelers stopping in for a meal or staying over.

Interestingly, there is another layer of lore.

Before Route 29 became a six-lane behemoth that hid the Wayside Inn behind a sound barrier in 2006, travelers could look over and see what was known far and wide as "that house with the candles in the windows." Explanations ranged from the house being haunted to a story about the mother of one of the owners' sons. Worried about him going off to the Civil War, she is said to have vowed to keep the candles burning until he came home—which, sadly, he never did. She continued burning the candles as a tribute to his patriotic sacrifice and her undying love for him.

The actual story behind the candles isn't quite as romantic, but it's still charming.

As Anglophiles and owners of the Cheshire Inn, the Hartkopfs are said to have revived the old English public-house tradition of putting lit candles in the windows of bedrooms that were available for rent. They put electric candles in all thirty-five windows and kept them burning twenty-four hours a day, extinguishing them only when the room was occupied—a distinction that got them a mention in *Ripley's Believe It or Not!*

But lighted candles aren't the only things that were flickering in the upstairs bedrooms of the Wayside Inn. Soon after the Baldersons closed on the property, a housekeeper who had worked for the previous owners and was staying on asked them if they had heard about the ghost.

They hadn't.

"Come with me," she said as she led the innkeepers to the second-floor bed chambers and pointed up at the ceiling. She said that often, when she was tidying up the rooms, she'd hear footsteps on the third floor and the sound of doors and drawers opening and shutting. She said she once saw a face peering out from the pattern in the bathroom wallpaper. A sensitive soul, the housekeeper definitely felt there was some kind of spirit in the house.

Then there were the questions over breakfast from the guests. "Is this house haunted?"

A couple recounted experiences of being awakened in the middle of the night by someone rattling the doorknob to their room so loudly that they felt compelled to get up and see who was there. Of course, it was no one. This happened night after night during their stay.

Some actually saw a materialized spirit, all describing it as the same woman with the same height and same hairstyle and dressed in servant's clothes. On one occasion, a friend who said she was a medium accompanied a guest for breakfast. The Baldersons asked if she'd like to meet the inn's resident ghost.

She said she would.

They took her upstairs and let her wander around alone for fifteen minutes or so. When she came downstairs, she said, "Oh, there's no ifs, ands or buts about it, you have a ghost."

The medium described the spirit as a woman between the ages of thirty-eight and forty-two. She was a cleaning lady who had passed away many years ago but didn't know she was dead. She stayed and simply continued to do her job in the house in the afterlife.

"Oh, and one more thing," the medium said, "her name is Jenny."

Perhaps the most disturbing phenomena guests in the house experienced was during the weekend after the 9/11 attacks. A couple had fled New York City for a quiet weekend to calm their nerves. The husband had worked in the World Trade Center but missed his ferry that day and so was spared.

They said nothing about a ghostly encounter at breakfast, but two weeks later, the Baldersons got an email from the wife, asking the questions they had so often gotten from guests. And then she told them what happened.

It wasn't the sounds of a doorknob rattling, footsteps walking above the bed or doors slamming in a distant hall. It was much more intense and urgent.

The woman said she had been awakened in the middle of the night, about 2:00 a.m., by someone pulling on her leg. She woke to see her leg uncovered and a servant woman grabbing it as if to tell her to wake up and get out of bed.

As startling as that supernatural manifestation was, it wasn't the most unsettling thing about the incident. When they returned to New York, the woman found out that her brother, who had gone camping in the Adirondacks that same weekend, had had an accident. He must have gotten up in the middle of the night and become disoriented making his way to the latrine.

The next day, he was found at the bottom of a nearby ravine. He was dead.

The woman felt that maybe her brother had come to her for help in the form of the servant specter who woke her in the middle of the night.

The phantom housekeeper continued to do her unseen chores until the innkeepers did some more major renovations on the house in 2004. This time, the project required the construction crew to cut through the exterior walls of the home.

After that, they never heard from Jenny again.

According to those in touch with the spirit world, cutting through the outside wall of a haunted house releases the unsettled entity from whatever earthly ties are holding them here. They are free to fully become part of the world beyond and be at peace.

Today, the house is quiet. Jenny's identity and the era she came from have never been determined. Her hard work on earth that continued after her death at the Wayside Inn is finally and forever done.

# PART IV

# NORTHERN NIGHTMARES

# 15

# SALOPHA

## SYKESVILLE

*Humble home transformed into a country estate*
*remains under the watchful eye of the Blue Lady.*

Sited on high ground surrounded by a grove of mature trees, this picturesque Gothic revival home at 691 River Road gets its name from "Salopia," one of the original land grants associated with the property. The word has its origins in the term *Salopian*, which refers to Shropshire on the Severn, a borough in western England on the border of Wales.

Later spellings of the name included "Salopia," "Solopia," "Solopha," "Saliopa" and "Salopha," the latter of which it's known by today. A house with a long and storied past peppered by the names of some of Howard County's most prominent families is home to the ghost of a woman who may have looked after them in life and stayed after death.

## THE HISTORY

Salopha stands on a tract of land known as "Belts Hills" that was laid out by forty-one-year-old John Belt Jr. on March 22, 1719. The son of John and Elizabeth Belt, he was born in West River and was married to Lucy Talbot Lawrence.

In 1722, John turned the property over to his younger brother Benjamin, who formally patented the eight hundred acres as "Belts Hills." Since part of the home that now comprises the kitchen and the two stories above it is thought to have been constructed around 1720, it may be that he and his wife, Elizabeth Middleton, built the lap-sided house. If they did, they didn't stay very long.

Just a few years later, in 1724, Benjamin sold the eight-hundred-acre "Belts Hills" property to John Taillour. Adjacent to Taillour's new home was a one-hundred-acre tract called "Salopia" that had been patented to John Johnson from the king of England in 1742.

The two properties were joined with Johnson's engagement to Talliour's only daughter, Margaret Higginson. A recent widow, Margaret's heart would be broken yet again by the untimely death of her fiancé before she could join him as his wife at "Salopia."

In 1744, Margaret sold the Belts Hills property and "improvements" to John Dorsey, the son of Edward Dorsey The sale price was one hundred pounds sterling.

A few years later, John Dorsey gave Belts Hills, the house and land to his twenty-four-year-old son Vachel Paul and his wife, Ruth, along with seven "negroes," perhaps as a wedding gift, in 1750. The enslaved peoples' names were recorded as Sam, Robin, James, Rose, Abigail, Samson of Rose and Fanney.

In 1752, Vachel expanded his land holdings by purchasing the one-hundred-acre "Saliopa" property from Margaret Higginson. He and Ruth then set about filling their new home with children. Son Levin was born in 1755, Vachel Jr. in 1760, Johnsa in 1762, Edward in 1762 and Elias in 1768. Their daughter Ruth was born in 1774.

The Dorseys expanded their home around 1769 by adding a dining room and a dining room entryway, an upstairs bedroom, a future bath and a hall.

On March 9, 1798, Vachel Paul Dorsey left this mortal world, turning over "Salopha" to his son Edward, thirty-six. The property remained in Edward's hands until 1802, when he sold it to Samuel and Richard Owings with the understanding that his mother, Ruth Dorsey, could stay in the house until she died.

At the time of her husband's death, Ruth was seventy years old. No one expected her to live much longer. But she did. In fact, she outlived her son Edward, who had relocated to Kentucky, where he died in 1804. She remained at the home until her death in 1814 at the age of eighty-six.

Begun in 1720, this greatly expanded Dorsey-Warfield home vibrates with supernatural activity. *Raymond and Patricia Emard Greenwald.*

By then, most of the Dorsey clan had relocated to Kentucky. Evidently, no one remembered the exact transaction. Several lawsuits regarding ownership of the property followed. After the legal dust settled, Samuel Owings was recognized as the owner of the property. On January 9, 1829, he gave the deed to Charles Warfield and his wife, Juliana Owings Dorsey, who was also Samuel's daughter and a Dorsey widow.

The couple had five sons together. Samuel Owings was born in 1825, Joshua Dorsey in 1831, Thomas Owings in 1835, Charles A. in 1837 and William Owings in 1840.

The same year his last son was born, Charles Warfield died. He left forty-three-year-old Julianna—now twice widowed—to raise their boys and run the farm. Her son Joshua, described as a "serious, hard-working planter," ended up taking over the reins, buying the property from his mother and brothers in 1863 for $8,000.

Joshua went on to marry Elizabeth Causey Polk. Together, they had five children: Lee Owings, Howard, Anna, Elizabeth "Bess" Polk and Nellie Polk. An unknown number of others died as infants.

Warfield took an active role in politics and served as a Howard County commissioner. He also had an eye for business and a taste for land. Between 1863 and 1886, he bought up fifteen pieces of land that ranged from 1 to 36 acres, bringing his total to 340 acres by the time he died on July 2, 1889. He was only fifty-eight.

After Joshua's burial at Springfield Cemetery in Sykesville, forty-two-year-old Elizabeth faced many of the same challenges as her widowed mother-in-law had. Fortunately, she was also blessed with industrious sons—and the business acumen she shared with her late husband.

They were rich.

Having three marriage-aged daughters, Elizabeth wanted to create a beautiful home where they could entertain worthy suitors and other guests.

It was at this time that they built the picturesque Gothic revival frame structure facing River Road that they connected to the south wall of the original home. It's said that the girls were taught to play the piano. A fiddler who came in on the 2:30 p.m. train from Baltimore frequently played in the parlor when the home was opened up for merriment and dancing.

On New Year's Day 1915, Elizabeth passed away, joining Joshua at Springfield Cemetery. By then, Anna and Nellie had been successfully married off. Their brother Lee Owings Warfield combined his inheritance with parts of the property he had bought up from his mother's heirs and came into possession of Salopha farm and its 335 acres.

A few years earlier, in 1912, Lee had married Eleanor Chinn Branch, the daughter of Reverend Henry Branch of the First Presbyterian Church in Ellicott City. They welcomed four children into their beautiful home in what was then known as West Friendship. Millicent was born in 1914, Lee Owings Jr. in 1917, Henry Branch in 1925 and Eleanor Chinn in 1927.

As a visiting minister at Springfield Presbyterian Church, Reverend Branch was a frequent visitor on the weekends. It's said that before his grandchildren were allowed to eat their Sunday pancakes, they had to recite a Bible verse to those at the breakfast table. The shortest verse in the Bible, "Jesus wept," was a favorite.

At the time, Salopha was an important dairy operation. The five-gallon and seven-and-a-half-gallon milk cans with brass plates inscribed with "Lee Warfield" had to be delivered and waiting at Gorsuch Switch Station by 7:14 a.m. each morning to be taken by train to Baltimore.

The Warfields continued to enjoy farm life until their sons shipped off to the navy for World War II and the work became too much for them. On February 25, 1943, they sold Salopha to William N. and Lockie Richardson.

From there, the farm changed hands many times. James D. and Bertha M. Brown purchased it in 1951. Harry A. Smuck and his wife, Thelma, bought it in 1954. Later that year, the Smucks sold it to John K. Eareckson and his wife.

The Earecksons reincarnated Salopha as the Circle X Ranch in partnership with Joseph Jelet and Grace Christopher, who moved into the house. Cabins on the property became a summer camp for youth. They brought in country music stars to perform as part of the *National Barn Dance* television show.

It was at this point that the nearly four-hundred-acre farm began to be carved up and parceled off. In 1962, the Christophers bought the house, barn and about twenty acres from the Earecksons. They changed the property name to Arrowhead and installed indoor plumbing.

The Christophers stayed there until Joseph died in September 1975. Grace then sold the property to James W. Dickey, a developer who built and sold homes on the property over the next four years. When he sold Salopha itself to John Gerard and Kathryn A. Westerfield on July 27, 1979, the property was down to 3.14 acres.

In 1984, the Westerfields sold the home and property to Lillian G. and Arthur S. Roemer for $158,000. The Roemers, who held craft shows in the barn, stayed until 1991, when they sold it to Raymond A. and Patricia E. Greenwald for $355,000.

The house the Greenwalds bought was perilously close to ruin. The foundation was practically gone. Poison ivy vines were growing through cracks in the walls in the library. Unfortunate past interior design choices had to be ripped out. The good news for Solpha was that the couple was more than up to the challenge

Now both retired, Pat as a Howard County teacher and Raymond as a physicist at Johns Hopkins University, the current owners rescued what was arguably a wreck of a house and lovingly renovated it into a literal showplace that has welcomed visitors on numerous historical home tours. Today, they live at Salopha in harmony with the present, at peace with the past and in the presence of a colorful spirit that looks after them and the home they love.

## THE HAUNTING

Like many old homes in Howard County, Salopha started out as a very simple structure that was added on to, renovated and reworked to suit the lifestyles and needs of whatever owner happened to reside there.

But while physical spaces change with the whims and desires of the living, the spectral world and the inhabitants eternally trapped in it remain to materialize in their old places as they once were, sometimes for centuries.

That seems to be the case with the spirit known as the "Blue Lady." It has appeared over the past three decades to the most recent owners, family and visitors to this historic home.

The first visitation came when the Greenwalds' daughters came to Maryland for spring break in 1991 to see their new home. Photos taken that day showed a strange blue form greeting the girls in the front hallway.

The older daughter initially stayed in a small room built in 1720. Waking one morning, she reported, "Mom, I talked to the Blue Lady all night! I know just what you should do with the kitchen."

The ghost roamed many of the rooms at Salopha. One time, when the owners' parents were staying in the bedroom that overlooks the terrace, a spectral form appeared to the owners' mother several times during the night. The father said he had the bruises from his wife's frightened midnight clutches to prove it.

The spirit felt at home downstairs, too. One evening at a dinner party in the newly restored dining room, one of the male guests reported sensing something very odd. A photograph of him in front of the fireplace revealed that he was right. The Blue Lady was standing next to him.

When the middle daughter got married in 1995, the wedding photographer took photos of the guests of honor as they walked into the barn. All of the photos taken before and after those of the mother and father of the bride were unremarkable. Theirs was anything but. There, walking into the barn between the Greenwalds, was the shiny blue apparition.

A few years later, the spirit appeared again. One night while sleeping alone in the house, the owner was awakened by the feeling that she was not alone. She slowly opened her eyes to see the specter of a woman standing at the foot of the bed.

This time, the ghost was dressed in pale green 1950s clothing, complete with a pillbox hat that sat neatly atop her pin-curled hairdo. The woman seemed to be speaking, but the owner heard nothing. Sometime during a fitful night of attempted sleep, the mysterious visitor disappeared.

The previous owners said they knew about the Blue Lady and thought she might have been a "mammy," because of what they perceived as her caring nature. Her kindliness aside, when she appeared to their son upstairs in the 1880s part of the house, the boy was so disturbed that he refused to sleep in his room. His parents brought in a priest to exorcise the house. The priest put a copper enamel plate on the door to keep the ghost out. It's not known if it worked.

The most dramatic manifestations came not too long ago, when the owner and her granddaughter were working on a sewing project in the third-floor craft room. They were sitting on the floor doing hand-stitching when both sewing machines in the room whirred to life, abruptly stopped and then started again.

Another time, the owner was sitting with her husband one Sunday evening as she was working on a lesson plan. Sensing something, she looked up to see a small pair of scissors fly off the top of the television five feet across the room onto the table next to her. Determined, she got up and put them back. They flew to her again. This time, she left them on the table. Somebody obviously thought she might need them.

Other odd occurrences attributed to the Blue Lady include the time the owner found everything that had been hanging on hooks in an alcove under the stairs neatly folded in piles in the hall. In another instance, three sets of curtains and valances in the bedroom were found on the bed—once again, neatly folded in a pile.

Whoever the Blue Lady is, she seems to be a benevolent and a rather tidy spirit. It's said that when the Dorseys moved west into Kentucky in the 1820s, they manumitted most of their enslaved people. The Blue Lady may have been one of the hardworking servants they left behind who faithfully continues to look after the living inhabitants of Salopha from beyond the grave.

# 16

# HOWARD LODGE

## SYKESVILLE

*Historic mansion turned total ruin comes back*
*to life as a welcoming home for the quick and the dead.*

A s one of the oldest and finest surviving plantation houses in Howard County, this imposing, five-level Greek revival brick home wears its nearly three-hundred-year history of triumphs and disasters like a comfortable cloak. Facing south at the top of a lovely knoll, the eighteenth-century Dorsey dwelling is located at 12301 Howard Lodge Drive in Sykesville.

Over the course of its long life, Howard Lodge has been given as a wedding gift, abused as a rental and resurrected as a showplace. It is home to nearly a half dozen restless wraiths that continue to watch, worry and walk its haunted halls.

## THE HISTORY

The historic home now known as Howard Lodge was originally sited on 1,500 acres of land granted by patent from Lord Baltimore to John Taillor (Taylor or Taillour) in 1727. The grant was known as "Taylors Park." Like the property referenced in the chapter on Salopha, it was inherited by Taillor's only daughter, Margaret Higginson.

Since neither Taillor nor Higginson lived on the property, the ramshackle cabins that probably dotted the land were likely rented out to tenant farmers. Shortly after her father died, Margaret divided the land into two parcels. In 1744, she sold roughly one half to John Dorsey and the other half to John Elder Jr.—both on the same day, and each for the sum of one hundred pounds sterling.

Born in Oxford, England, in 1688, John Dorsey, who had married Honor Stafford Elder in 1708, was described in the deed for the property as a "Maryland planter." The Dorseys were absentee landlords. They lived on their home plantation on a tract of land known as "First Discovery" near Elkridge.

In 1750, John Dorsey gave his son Edward John the 740 acres of "Taylors Park" that he had purchased in 1744, along with seven enslaved people, some of whose names were Jack, Toby, Charles, Hagar and Jenny. Since Edward had married Elizabeth "Betty" Gillis on July 29, 1750, the property was likely given as a wedding gift to set the newlyweds up on their own plantation.

The exact date of Howard Lodge's construction isn't known, but it's been estimated that it was sometime in the 1750s. It was an exceptionally grand home, especially for the time.

Built of Flemish and English bond brick ballast, the home had an impressive center passage, forty-seven feet and eight inches long by thirty-

Shown with its now-removed porch, this grand manor is haunted by watchful and worried entities. *Howard County Historical Society.*

five feet, four inches deep. Dorsey decked out the gable-roofed home with rich wood-paneled walls, fancy dentil cornices, display cupboards, corner fireplaces and many other fine features. Like most homes of the time, the kitchen was a separate log building to the rear of the house. At the time it was built, Howard Lodge easily rivaled Belmont and Waverly, which were constructed by other members of the Dorsey family during that period.

Edward and Betty set about filling their newly built residence with children. Ezekiel John was born in 1751, Joseph in 1754, Edward Hill "Hillary" in 1760 and Henry "Harry" in 1768.

Although the land he lived on was farmed, Edward was a merchant by trade who did a little banking as well. He loaned money to planters in what was then Anne Arundel County. The loans were secured with the value of their enslaved people, livestock and personal property.

After the Revolutionary War, when Baltimore began to grow, Edward may have relocated to the city or another farm. Tax records in 1783 show that his son Edward "Hill" Dorsey Jr. was assessed for 740 acres of "Taylors Park" and other properties as well as eight enslaved people, twenty cattle, twelve sheep and seven horses.

Edward Jr. had married Deborah MacCubbin in 1781, so Edward Sr., like his father before him, likely set his son up at Howard Lodge. Plantation life apparently didn't agree with them, because they didn't stay long. Records show that only one of their sons, Edward Hill, was born in Queen Caroline Parrish, Anne Arundel County (now Howard County) in 1795. The other five sons and daughters were born in Baltimore City.

By 1798, Edward Jr. had rented out the property to several tenant farmers. At that time, a man named Henry Carter was living in the Howard Lodge house.

Twenty-six years later, in 1824, Edward Jr. sold four hundred acres of land to his son Samuel for just ten dollars. Like his father and grandfather before him, Samuel probably received the property as a wedding gift. He married Mary Wilkins in 1821.

In 1831, Samuel patented 350 acres of the property as "Piney Grove." A few years later, in 1837, Edward Jr. sold the Howard Lodge house to Samuel for $200 a year for the rest of his life. Edward died in 1839, and Samuel inherited the property.

In April 1854, Samuel advertised the property for sale, noting:

> *530 of the 930 acres of the farm were cleared, with the rest in wood, and with meadows in timothy. There were apple and peach orchards and a*

*garden supplied with fruit and some fine grapes, and a tastefully ornamented lawn. The buildings on the farm were described as a large double brick house, with stone kitchen attached, dairy, meat-house, ice house, granary, corn house, barn, stabling, and quarters for slaves.*

Unfortunately, the farm didn't sell.

The man handling the sale, William W. Glenn of Baltimore, ended up buying it from Samuel for $23,250 in 1856. William turned around and sold it to his brother John. Since he already had a summer home at "Hilton" in Catonsville, John didn't live at Howard Lodge. He kept it as an investment.

Francis Scott Key Jr., whose poet father was the author of "The Star-Spangled Banner," and his wife, Elizabeth Lloyd, tried to buy the property. Records show that they at least lived in the vicinity of Howard Lodge, but it's not known if they actually occupied the house. Sadly, the Keys got into financial difficulties. Glenn sued them for nonpayment and repossessed the property in 1861. He then sold Howard Lodge to Thomas Gerven of New York. Gerven was as financially unlucky as Key and lost the house to foreclosure in 1869. Glenn then reacquired the property at a public auction.

After those two home sale catastrophes, Glenn finally sold Howard Lodge to fifty-five-year-old Theodore Mottu, a Baltimore lumber dealer, in 1876. It was about that time that the home was named Howard Lodge, perhaps because it was used as a country home/hunting lodge and was located in Howard County. Although Mottu passed away in 1896, the property remained in the family until May 7, 1907, when his estate sold it to William Wilson for $16,800.

In 1917, the B.F. Shriver Canning Company purchased the property and placed tenant farmers on the land to grow vegetables for canning. Twenty-three years later, in 1940, the company sold Howard Lodge to John H. and Myrtle A. Bobst on what was likely a much smaller piece of property.

On March 15, 1943, the Bobsts sold the property to Arthur Justus and Mildred Lauer Linn. At the time, Arthur was employed at Hamilton National Bank in Washington, D.C. The couple lived with their daughters Lois, Jane and Elinor and son Arthur Jr. in University Park, along with Mildred's mother, Dora. The Howard Lodge property was likely a weekend or summer property for the family.

The Bobsts stayed for nearly ten years. Adam and Anna G. Stotsky bought the property on July 10, 1952, and kept it until November 3, 1959, when they sold the home and its two hundred acres to Roy F. Emery and his wife, Jacqueline Marchal.

A lawyer by trade as well as a land developer, Roy Emery was known as one of the more colorful members of the Howard County bar. He often read his poetry to fellow lawyers. The couple and their three children—daughters Ariane and Lynn and son Christopher—had moved to Howard Lodge from Cooksville, where they had been operating a dairy farm.

According to Jacqueline, the house endured many years of neglect and had been inhabited by rats, pigs and "hillbillies" before they moved in. Born as Countess Jacqueline Marchal de Beauregard, she had an eye for the finer things in life. Over the years, Jacqueline worked tirelessly to restore the home and fill it with continental and American antiques.

Although the couple divorced in 1971, Jacqueline stayed in the home. She married Curtis J. Streeter a short time later. But she felt her time at Howard Lodge was over. On July 20, 1973, she said goodbye to the home she had so lovingly restored, selling it to Luke Edward Terry Jr. and his wife, Jane Brower Terry.

Tragically, less than six months later, Jacqueline said goodbye to her new husband, too. Curtis Streeter died on January 5, 1974, and was buried at St. John's Cemetery in Ellicott City. He was forty-four years old.

The Terrys were both doctors, Luke a doctor of internal medicine and Jane a psychiatrist. They stayed at Howard Lodge for nearly forty years, selling it on its fifteen remaining acres for $940,000 on June 28, 2010. The new master and mistresses of the manor were Dr. Bernard J. Rauscher, an experimental astrophysicist at NASA; his wife, Francesca Galbani; and her sister Nicoletta Galbani.

In 2011, the Raucher-Galbanis petitioned the U.S. National Park Service to put the home in the National Register of Historic Places. On October 9, 2012, Howard Lodge, with its nearly 360-year history and unexplained haunted mysteries, was added to the register, securing a permanent place of honor on Howard County's list of nationally recognized landmarks.

# THE HAUNTING

A house that has seen nearly three centuries of life and death and remains to tell its story is remarkable in and of itself. So are the owners and visitors who are open enough to listen and value it.

While it's unknown how many past inhabitants of Howard Lodge encountered ghosts, there are compelling accounts of the supernatural from recent owners, most notably from Jacqueline Emery.

In 1967, she invited Hans Holzer, an Austrian parapsychologist who wrote more than 140 books on ghosts, the afterlife, witchcraft, extraterrestrial beings and other phenomena, to visit Howard Lodge.

The famed paranormal investigator came to interview Jacqueline about the home and her paranormal experiences in 1969. Earlier, she'd had a pair of sensitive visitors tell her that there were a total of five spirits in the house.

Holzer recounted what Jacqueline told him in his book *The Ghosts That Walk in Washington*. "Three years ago, I became aware of a man on the landing. I know it is a man although I have never seen him. I'm absolutely convinced that he's a man either in his late forties or early fifties, and in addition, he's from the eighteenth century because in my mind's eye I can see him."

Jacqueline also reported hearing footsteps on the stairs, a foggy mist on the landing and in other rooms and strange smells that were somehow familiar. And then there was the spirit of the baby. "I heard breathing. It was in the master bedroom…the breathing came from the right side of the bed, below, as if a child would have slept in a trundle bed.…There's not a mother in the world who will not recognize the breathing of a child when it's sick and has a fever.…That child cries and has pain."

She also felt that a woman was there, "on my side of the bed.…I'm sure she slept on the right because the child is on the right."

Jacqueline also spoke of the dogs barking at nothing and a rocking chair that rocked on its own. Some family members saw a phantom boy in the yard. Others heard the sound of silverware being gathered up in the dining room. Most unnerving was the son and, later, the paranormal investigator encountering a malevolent spirit in the basement that once was heard saying, "You are standing on my grave."

However, on the whole, Jaqueline and the children felt that the home had a calm, positive feeling. So, during Jaqueline's interview with Holzer, as the conversation continued and accounts spilled out, the famed paranormal investigator evidently offered to have a medium spiritually cleanse the home and release the entities that seemed to be trapped there.

Jacqueline abruptly ended the interview.

Coming from Europe, she was comfortable living with the lingering spirits of the long dead. She felt they had as much right to be in the house as she and her family did. So, the "ghost hunter" packed up and left. The spirits stayed at Howard Lodge, where they likely remain to this day.

# BIBLIOGRAPHY

## Books

Boyd, Thomas H. *The History of Montgomery County Maryland, from its earliest settlement in 1650 to 1879....* Baltimore, MD: W.K. Boyle & Son, Printers, 1879.

Cramm, Joetta M. *A Pictorial History of Howard County*. Norfolk, VA: Donning Company, 1987.

Feaga, Barbara W. *Howard's Roads to the Past*. Ellicott City, MD: Howard County Sesquicentennial Celebration Committee, 2001.

Gallager, Trish. *Ghosts & Haunted Houses of Maryland*. Centerville, MD: Tidewater Publishers, 1988

Hammond, John Martin. *Colonial Mansions of Maryland and Delaware*. Philadelphia and London: J.B. Lippencott Company, 1914.

Holland, Celia M. *Old Homes and Families of Howard County, Maryland*. N.p.: self-published, 1987.

———. *Ellicott City, Mill Town, U.S.A.* Updated by Janet P. Kusterer and Charlotte T. Holland. Ellicott City, MD: Historic Ellicott City Inc., 2003.

Holzer, Hans. *The Ghosts That Walk in Washington*. New York: Doubleday, 1971.

Howard County Historical Society. *Images of America: Howard County*. Charleston, SC: Arcadia Publishing, 2011.

Okonowicz, Ed. *The Big Book of Maryland Ghost Stories*. Lanham, MD: Globe Pequot, 2010.

Sharp, Henry K. *The Patapsco River Valley, Cradle of the Industrial Revolution in Maryland*. Baltimore: Maryland Historical Society, 2001.

Wilstach, Paul. *Tidewater Maryland*. Indianapolis, IN: Bobbs-Merrill, 1931.

## Selected Online Sources

An American Family History. "Burgess Family." https://www.anamericanfamilyhistory.com.

Ancestry. com. https://www.ancestry.com.

Autumn Walk at Emerson. "Santa Heim, Merrieland (aka Savage, MD)." http://www.autumnwalk.com.

Early Colonial Settlers of Southern Maryland and Virginia. https://www.colonial-settlers-md-va.us/index.php.

Elkridge Heritage Society. "Collection Research: Land Owners & Patents, 1670–1812." http://www.elkridgeheritage.org.

"A Few Odd Moments in Howard County: Patapsco Female Institute." YouTube. https://www.youtube.com.

Find a Grave. https://www.findagrave.com.

Haunted Road Media. "Haunted Belmont Manor Ghost Stories with Psychic Medium Rob Gutro!" https://www.hauntedroadmedia.com.

Howard County Conservancy. "History—Belmont." https://www.howardnature.org.

Justia. "Olivia v. State." https://law.justia.com.

Maryland Department of Assessments and Taxation. Real Property Data Search. https://sdat.dat.maryland.gov.

Maryland Historical Trust. "Maryland Inventory of Historic Properties (MIHP)." https://mht.maryland.gov.

Maryland Paranormal Research. "Haunted Savage Mill Maryland." https://blog.maryland-paranormal.com.

MDLANDREC. Maryland State Archives. https://mdlandrec.net/main.

Meetup. "Investigation at Belmont Manor and Historic Park." https://www.meetup.com.

MidAtlantic Day Trips. "Ghost Hunting at Belmont Manor." http://www.midatlanticdaytrips.com.

———. "The Ghosts of Historic Savage Mill." http://www.midatlanticdaytrips.com.

On-Line Buzzletter. "Our Ghost Investigator at Belmont Manor." http://rob-tom-dolly-franklin.blogspot.com.

Patapsco. "Elkridge." https://patapsco.org.

Rob Gutro's Paranormal Blog. http://ghostsandspiritsinsights.blogspot.com.

Useless Information. "Christmas Time in Santa Heim." https://uselessinformation.org.

Wikipedia. https://en.wikipedia.org.

WUSA9. "Belmont's Haunted Mansion." January 23, 2017. https://www.wusa9.com.

## Selected Articles

Bienvenu, Justin, "The Difference between a Residual and Intelligent Haunting." Medium. 2019. https://medium.com.

Freed, Eric. "The Ghost Walk in Historic Savage Mill." Away from the Things of Man. September 29, 2014. https://www.awayfromthethingsofman.com.

Gulley, Rosemary Ellen. "Iron in Ghost Lore." Occult World. 2007. https://occult-world.com.

Historic England. "What Are Witch's Marks?" https://historicengland.org.uk.

Lyons, Sheridan. "Officer Tells of Finding Body as Baxter Trial Opens." *Baltimore Sun*, April 29, 1981.

McDonald, Allan. "Horrible Health and Safety Histories: Child Labor Amalgamate 2018." http://www.amalgamate-safety.com.

McGill, John. "The MacGill-McGill Family of Maryland 1537–1948." http://wvancestry.com/ReferenceMaterial/Files/The_MacGill_-_McGill_Family_of_Maryland.pdf.

Powell, Lisa. "Life Returns to the Dead of Belmont—Elkridge Maryland." Southern Spirit Guide. April 7, 2016. http://www.southernspiritguide.org.

Ricksecker, Mike. "Paranormal Roads: Haunted Belmont Manor." YouTube. https://www.youtube.com/watch?v=XXoZciwOjgk.

US Department of Labor Statistics. "History of Children Working in the United States—Part 1: Little Children Working." January 2017. https://www.bls.gov.

## Other

Nesbitt, Jennifer Chandler. "Beneath the Surface." Unpublished manuscript. Chestertown, Maryland. Fall 2015.

Xeroxed article on "The Vineyard." Avoca Folder—Vertical Files at the Howard County Historical Society Archives.

# About the Author

A fter spending more than twenty years living in, learning about and immersing herself in the history of Howard County as a past president, officer and board member of the Howard County Historical Society and board member of Historic Ellicott City Inc., author Shelley Davies Wygant is pleased to add *Haunted Howard County* to her library of local history titles. Her earlier works include *Images of America: Howard County* and *Haunted Ellicott City*. An advertising creative director and copywriter for Wygant & Co., she currently makes her home in Sewickley, Pennsylvania, where she serves on the board of Neville House Associates, custodians of Woodville, a National Historic Landmark and Whiskey Rebellion site. She, her husband, Jeffrey, and Willow, their Treeing Walker Coonhound, live in a historic—but not haunted—house close to family and the city of Pittsburgh.